Global Journalism Collaborations

Global Journalism Collaborations offers guidance on detailed ways to create collaborative international projects in the communications and journalism fields – a hot topic in higher education.

The chapters are contributed by professors and journalists from around the world. The authors explain, step-by-step, the process of collaborating with students and instructors at universities in dozens of countries in order to produce digital storytelling projects that are streamed worldwide. The book will inspire academics and students in any discipline to develop and create their own collaborative projects by sharing lessons learned through case studies of successful global collaborations.

This truly interdisciplinary work will interest scholars and instructors of journalism, media studies, mass communication, higher education and anyone working on collaborative projects across a variety of disciplines.

Katherine C. Blair is an Associate Professor of Broadcast Journalism at Leeds Trinity University, UK where she has taught television and social media journalism for 16 years. Before that, she was a television presenter, reporter, producer and director at ITV Yorkshire, CBC in Newfoundland and Labrador and MCTV in Timmins Canada for 20 years.

Marion Coomey is a Professor in the RTA School of Media at Toronto Metropolitan University in Toronto, Canada. She teaches international media production, broadcast presentation and writing. Marion has been a news reporter, host, writer and producer at CBC TV and Radio across Canada. She is Executive Producer of Global Campus Studio Productions, a project bringing together students from 15 countries to produce online shows.

Faith Sidlow is the chair of the Media, Communications and Journalism Department at California State University, Fresno, and associate professor of broadcast and multimedia journalism. She is an award-winning broadcast journalist with 30 years experience in TV and radio news. Faith worked as a reporter, anchor and producer for the Fresno NBC affiliate for 28 years. Her early broadcast career included radio reporter and board operator at KPBS-FM; San Diego reporter for KNX News Radio, Los Angeles and research intern for CBS News in London.

Routledge Focus on Journalism Studies

Front-Page Scotland
Newspapers and the Scottish Independence Referendum
David Patrick

Public Television in Poland
Political Pressure and Public Service Media in a Post-communist Country
Agnieszka Węglińska

Election Politics and the Mass Press in Long Edwardian Britain
Christopher Shoop-Worrall

Journalism's Racial Reckoning
The News Media's Pivot to Diversity and Inclusion
Brad Clark

Re-examining the UK Newspaper Industry
Marc Edge

Humanitarian Journalists
Covering Crises from a Boundary Zone
Martin Scott, Kate Wright, and Mel Bunce

Constructive Journalism:
Precedents, Principles, and Practices
Peter Bro

Global Journalism Collaborations
Worldwide Storytelling Projects in Higher Education
Edited by Katherine C. Blair, Marion Coomey and Faith Sidlow

For more information about this series, please visit: www.routledge.com/Routledge-Handbooks-in-Religion/book-series

Global Journalism Collaborations
Worldwide Storytelling Projects in Higher Education

Edited by
Katherine C. Blair, Marion Coomey
and Faith Sidlow

LONDON AND NEW YORK

First published 2024

by Routledge

4 Park Square, Milton Park, Abingdon, Oxon OX14 4RN

and by Routledge

605 Third Avenue, New York, NY 10158

Routledge is an imprint of the Taylor & Francis Group, an informa business

© 2024 selection and editorial matter, Katherine C. Blair, Marion Coomey and Faith Sidlow; individual chapters, the contributors

The right of Katherine C. Blair, Marion Coomey and Faith Sidlow to be identified as the authors of the editorial material, and of the authors for their individual chapters, has been asserted in accordance with sections 77 and 78 of the Copyright, Designs and Patents Act 1988.

All rights reserved. No part of this book may be reprinted or reproduced or utilised in any form or by any electronic, mechanical, or other means, now known or hereafter invented, including photocopying and recording, or in any information storage or retrieval system, without permission in writing from the publishers.

Trademark notice: Product or corporate names may be trademarks or registered trademarks, and are used only for identification and explanation without intent to infringe.

British Library Cataloguing-in-Publication Data
A catalogue record for this book is available from the British Library

Library of Congress Cataloging-in-Publication Data
Names: Blair, Katherine, editor. | Coomey, Marion, editor. | Sidlow, Faith, editor.
Title: Global journalism collaborations: worldwide storytelling projects in higher education / edited by Katherine Blair, Marion Coomey, Faith Sidlow.
Description: Abingdon, Oxon; New York, NY: Routledge, 2024. | Series: Routledge focus on journalism studies | Includes bibliographical references and index.
Identifiers: LCCN 2023055837 (print) | LCCN 2023055838 (ebook) | ISBN 9781032550411 (hardback) | ISBN 9781032550428 (paperback) | ISBN 9781003428725 (ebook)
Subjects: LCSH: Journalism—Study and teaching. | Collaborative journalism—Study and teaching. | Intercultural communication—Study and teaching. | LCGFT: Essays.
Classification: LCC PN4785 .G57 2024 (print) | LCC PN4785 (ebook) | DDC 070.407—dc23/eng/20231221
LC record available at https://lccn.loc.gov/2023055837
LC ebook record available at https://lccn.loc.gov/2023055838

ISBN: 978-1-032-55041-1 (hbk)
ISBN: 978-1-032-55042-8 (pbk)
ISBN: 978-1-003-42872-5 (ebk)

DOI: 10.4324/9781003428725

Typeset in Times New Roman
by codeMantra

We dedicate this book to our students who inspire us and our colleagues who believe we should continue to strive for more.

Contents

List of contributors ix
Foreword xi

Introduction 1
FAITH SIDLOW

1 **The big picture** 5
NICK DUARTE

2 **Student engagement: How the Global News Relay began** 14
SARAH JONES

3 **Global News Relay (GNR) 2.0** 22
FAITH SIDLOW AND KATHERINE C. BLAIR

4 **Global Campus Studio Productions (GCSP)** 34
MARION COOMEY

5 **The Global Pop-Up Newsroom** 43
DAVID BAINES AND DEVADAS RAJARAM

6 **Global E-News Immersion Initiative (GENII)** 50
PRIYA RAJASEKAR

7 **Global Reporting Program (GRP)** 57
PETER KLEIN AND BRITNEY DENNISON

8 **Student perspectives** 65
KATHERINE C. BLAIR

9	**Instructor feedback** MARION COOMEY	75
10	**Technology: Getting it right** MARION COOMEY	85
11	**The challenges of an uneven playing field** SYLVIA VOLLENHOVEN	95
12	**Industry: How the pros do it** FAITH SIDLOW AND KATHERINE C. BLAIR	103
13	**Lessons learned** KATHERINE C. BLAIR, MARION COOMEY AND FAITH SIDLOW	113
14	**Still to come…** KATHERINE C. BLAIR, MARION COOMEY AND FAITH SIDLOW	119
	Index	*127*

Contributors

David Baines
Newcastle University
UK

Senior lecturer in journalism, who worked for 30 years on regional newspapers. His research relates to journalism and communities; transformations in journalism work, roles and practices and journalism ethics and diversity and journalism.

Britney Dennison
University of British Columbia (UBC)
Canada

Executive editor of the Global Reporting Centre. Instructor for the Global Reporting Program at the UBC School of Journalism, Writing, and Media. She has won Edward R. Murrow awards, an Online Journalism award and a Canadian Association of Journalists award. Her work has appeared on NBC News, PBS NewsHour, the *Toronto Star* and more.

Nick Duarte
Toronto Metropolitan University (TMU)
Canada

Writer, educator and researcher. He holds an MA in Media Production from TMU. He has taught in the MA Media Production program at TMU and has worked as an eCurriculum Specialist, developing engaging online learning programs. Nicholas has also worked as a development producer, graphic designer and social media coordinator.

Sarah Jones
University of Gloucestershire
UK

Professor of Education Innovation and Pro Vice Chancellor at the University of Gloucestershire, UK. After nearly a decade in television news, Sarah began working in universities focusing on future media, future technology and future education. Sarah holds a PhD in Immersive Storytelling and has published extensively on virtual and augmented reality.

Peter Klein
University of British Columbia (UBC)
Canada

Executive editor of investigations at NBC News. Professor and former director of the UBC School of Journalism, Writing, and Media. Former executive director of the Global Reporting Centre. Former producer of CBS News 60 Minutes. Peter has three Emmys and numerous other journalism awards.

Devadas Rajaram
Alliance University
Bangalore, India

Professor of New Media at Alliance University in Bangalore, India. Devadas heads the Media Innovation Lab, where he focuses on immersive storytelling with AR, VR and XR technologies, AI and Gamification. He was a pioneer in digital journalism, who began experimenting with mobile storytelling in 1997.

Priya Rajasekar
Cambridge Institute for Sustainability, Leadership
UK

Program manager for eLearning, Cambridge Institute for Sustainability Leadership, and a freelance journalist and columnist. Previously, Priya worked as an assistant professor in multiplatform journalism at Coventry University in Coventry, UK and as an associate professor of digital journalism at the Asian College of Journalism in Chennai, India.

Sylvia Vollenhoven
University of Johannesburg (UJ)
South Africa

Professor of Practice, Department of Communications and Media. Sylvia is a writer, award-winning journalist, playwright, filmmaker and founder of Vision in Africa that has spearheaded innovative international training initiatives and creative productions. Lead trainer for the Thomas Foundation's (UK) first-ever documentary filmmaking course at Cardiff University.

Foreword

The idea for this book started from an international conference called Global Collaborations held online in November 2021. The conference brought together many of those whose chapters appear in this book as well as many more educators who are passionate about using international collaborations as a way of bringing out the best in our students.

Creating international collaborative projects on top of teaching skills and educating our students is not an easy option. It takes more time, an adaptable internal body clock and dedication above and beyond. The reason we do it is because we recognise the very positive benefits for our students. Quite simply, the extra work, the long hours and the endless complications just seem worth it.

We thank each and every author, student and industry professional who has contributed to this book. We are eternally grateful for your thoughts, ideas, time and generosity. Beyond the academics, we can't thank enough the technical people and staff who have made it all happen. We know that the chocolate biscuits, bottle of something or coffee runs were never sufficient to thank you for all the hours you put in.

And we thank all the students who challenge us, force us to think creatively and provide us with a reason to do the best we can each and every day.

Introduction

Faith Sidlow

Figure 0.1 Global Campus Studio Productions hosts, Leeds Trinity University, UK.

In April 2017, I attended the annual national Broadcast Education Association conference in Las Vegas, Nevada. As I thumbed through the sessions being offered, I found one called "Google News Lab and Global Campus Network: The democratization of digital tools and techniques across borders and communities" (beaweb.org, 2017).

Intrigued by the title, I was excited to attend the session as I had been running a program called Global News Relay at my university from California since 2015.

The session was led by Professor Rick Grunberg from the RTA School of Media at Ryerson University (now Toronto Metropolitan University) in Toronto, Canada, which he billed as a one-of-a-kind global collaboration among universities. After the session, I introduced myself to Rick and informed him that the Global News Relay had been running since 2014, initiated by

DOI: 10.4324/9781003428725-1

Dr. Sarah Jones at Coventry University in England (Chapter 3). As we sat by the hotel pool and chatted over drinks, Rick phoned his colleague, the director of the Global Campus Network program (as it was called at the time), in Toronto whom he referred to as my Canadian counterpart. This chance encounter led to a valuable collaboration between Marion Coomey and me, where my students participated in her Global Campus Studio projects (Chapter 2) and her students participated in my Global News Relay (Chapter 4).

I was already collaborating with other contributors to this book including Priya Rajasekar from Coventry University, who I met virtually during the Global News Relay in 2015. The following year, Priya recruited my California students into her pilot program for the Global News Immersion Lab (GNIL), which later became the Global E-News Immersion Initiative (GENII), an international virtual news gathering production by student journalists from the UK, Germany, Lebanon, and California, U.S. (Chapter 6).

Before joining Coventry, Priya was a lecturer at the Asian College of Journalism in Chennai, India, where she collaborated with Dr. Melissa Wall from Cal State Northridge and Dr. David Baines from Newcastle University on a project called the Global Pop-Up Newsroom (Chapter 5). This project began in 2012 when Melissa's students used cell phones and Twitter to cover an event in Los Angeles.

Pop-up Newsroom turned global in 2013 to include Priya's students in India, David's students in the UK, and Melissa's students in California, along with others in Taiwan, to report on economic inequality over a 24-hour period. Students uploaded their stories to a temporary Global Pop-Up news website, RebelMouse, and Twitter.

Priya joined the first Global News Relay at Coventry University in 2014, along with David and his students at Newcastle, Devadas Rajaram and his students from American University Bulgaria (AUBG) and a half dozen other universities (Chapter 2).

After the successful completion of the GENII pilot in 2016, Priya expanded the initiative and recruited Dev, who had returned to the Asian College of Journalism in Chennai and Elizabeth Müller from the Media University in Stuttgart, Germany.

Global Campus Studio in Toronto was in full swing with more than a dozen universities participating. Students chose themes that were newsworthy and relevant around the world, but instead of covering them over a 24-hour period, they produced 20 to 60-minute current affairs programs. Some shows were streamed live. Others were recorded and posted to YouTube and Facebook. The programs were co-hosted by students from each university and showcased short videos produced at each location. The goal was for the students to interact with one another throughout the shows to share their views and opinions on the chosen themes.

Global Pop-Up Newsroom expanded to cover global stories, including International Women's Day and the Climate Crisis, with universities throughout

Europe, Asia and Africa. Professional and citizen journalists were invited to participate with the student journalists.

The Global News Relay also gained momentum. Students at Fresno State in California hosted five-hour-long programs with students from 17 universities in 10 countries in 2017 and 2018 on topics ranging from solutions journalism to homelessness and poverty.

Hong Kong Baptist University took over hosting duties from 2019 to 2021, and in 2022, Katherine Blair and her students at Leeds Trinity University in the UK hosted a Global News Relay show, *Mind Matters*. I had already met Katherine virtually in 2019 when she launched *World Earth Day Live!*—a global broadcast news collaboration to coincide with the 50th anniversary of World Earth Day.

While journalism education is traditionally practice based, it is less known for researching and publishing on topics such as this kind of immersive experiential learning, but Nicholas Duarte rounds up much of the literature in this area (Chapter 1).

Many of the case studies are projects that are shoehorned into the rest of the curriculum; however, in British Columbia, Canada, the sole focus of one of their courses is on Global Reporting (Chapter 7).

We have witnessed the benefit to students who participate in these projects. They get hands-on experience in journalism and news production, which helps them develop their skills and hone their craft. They also have the opportunity to work with students and faculty from other universities in countries far, far away, which broadens their perspectives and exposes them to new and different cultures.

This kind of international collaboration helps students develop cross-cultural communication skills. The programs also offer students a unique learning experience that goes beyond the traditional classroom setting and provides them with the opportunity to work on projects that have real-world impact. The global network of universities that participates in these programs provides students with a rich and diverse network of contacts, which they can tap into as they move forward in their careers.

Significant effort is invested in creating innovative, engaging and fun teaching methods, driven by the tremendous value students derive from them (Chapter 8). Consequently, instructors willingly dedicate additional time and effort to make sure their students receive the maximum benefits from these projects (Chapter 9).

The primary objective of journalism education is to produce graduates who are able to seamlessly transition into the industry. Consequently, we assess whether these types of collaborative projects align with industry expectations and standards (Chapter 12).

While recognizing the challenges (Chapter 11), as well as the improvements in technology (Chapter 10), which help make such projects possible, we share what we, the authors, have learned while leading these projects

(Chapter 13) and where these global collaborations in higher education might go in the future (Chapter 14).

Katherine, Marion and I are all committed to ensuring these projects continue, even when we and other instructors and tutors are not here to lead them. This book encapsulates the core concept of empowering fellow educators to create similar programs and keep global collaborations alive.

We want to share our collective experience and expertise and inspire others to engage in collaborative journalism initiatives that help promote and enhance journalism education. We hope that this book serves as a valuable resource for educators, journalists and students by offering a comprehensive overview of collaborative journalism programs and outlining the steps and strategies needed to successfully establish similar programs at other universities. We hope this book also serves as a guide for other disciplines seeking to internationalize their curriculum through virtual assignments.

References

Google News Lab and Global Campus Network: The democratization of digital tools and techniques across borders and communities. (2017). *beaweb.org*. Retrieved from http://www.beaweb.org/pdfs/BEA2017CP.pdf

1 The big picture

Nick Duarte

Figure 1.1 Global Campus Studio Productions, Leeds Trinity University, UK.

In recent decades, there has been a significant shift towards the internationalization of postsecondary education (PSE) or higher education (HE). In 2018, the Association of Universities and Colleges of Canada found that more than 90% of its members mentioned internationalization in their mission/strategic plans (Marinoni, 2019, p. 25).

The recent prioritization of internationalization strategies has been motivated by factors such as globalization, universities' quest for competitive advantage (Adapa, 2013) and the burgeoning demand for 21st-century skills (Hilliker & Loranc, 2021; Kolm et al., 2022) and global competencies (Taras et al., 2013).

A broad spectrum of approaches, ranging from international research collaborations to the incorporation of international students into domestic programs, the development of joint degrees and international conferences, can be employed by universities to internationalize their research and education (Adapa, 2013). However, these strategies are not universally applicable; they vary according to each institution's unique economic and political circumstances, rationales and incentives (Adapa, 2013).

Despite their numerous advantages, some strategies can be challenging to implement. For example, study abroad programs use experiential learning to facilitate cultural immersion and develop students' intercultural competencies (Taras et al., 2013). These programs often prove costly for students (Hilliker & Loranc, 2022; O'Dowd, 2021; Antonopoulou, 2019; Bowen et al., 2021; Taras et al., 2013) and suffer from a shortage of robust funding options (Bowen et al., 2019; McCullough et al., 2019). Furthermore, the COVID-19 pandemic imposed campus shutdowns and travel restrictions, exacerbating barriers to physical interaction (Sierra et al., 2022; Kolm et al., 2022). The challenges posed by in-person internationalization strategies have expedited the adoption of Internet communication technologies (ICTs) for internationalization purposes (Sierra et al., 2022; Kolm et al., 2022).

The advent and widespread adoption of powerful ICTs have effectively dismantled communication barriers and facilitated seamless collaboration among students and faculty across borders (Middleweek et al., 2020; Hénard et al., 2012). The global journalism collaboration projects discussed throughout this book have harnessed ICTs to internationalize journalism education in an accessible and cost-effective way.

This chapter will broadly examine the various dimensions, challenges and implications of global journalism collaboration (GJC) projects and position them within a subset of internationalization strategies called virtual exchange (VE).

Defining virtual exchange and global journalism collaboration

Within VE environments, learners engage in collaborative online interaction with international "partners from diverse cultural contexts and geographical locations" (O'Dowd, 2021). These interactions occur within the context of coursework and are supervised by educators (O'Dowd, 2021; Sierra et al., 2022). Through sustained periods of interaction, VE aims to foster a deeper understanding of different cultural perspectives (Ferreira-Lopes et al., 2021; Hilliker & Loranc, 2021; O'Dowd, 2021), challenge cultural stereotypes (Albeanu, 2016) and improve students' comfort with online interaction (Hilliker & Loranc, 2021). The crux of VE programs is collaboration, allowing students to work together to achieve a common goal (Askari et al., 2022).

Although the original purpose of VE was to support foreign language education, the broad appeal of its use cases has made it a popular educational tool across other domains. VE strategies have been used to teach public policy (Sierra et al., 2022), marketing (Higgins et al., 2013), education (Hilliker & Loranc, 2021), business (Taras et al., 2013; Ferreira-Lopes et al., 2021), biomedical engineering (McCullough et al., 2019), global health (Bowen et al., 2021) and, of course, journalism (Bowen et al., 2019; Askari et al., 2022)

The role of foreign correspondents, the rigour of international reporting (Bowen et al., 2019) and the success of "large-scale industry collaborations such as the Panama and Paradise Papers" (Middleweek et al., 2020) have driven the adoption of journalism education that has an international focus. Congruently, the challenges of travel costs and the COVID-19 pandemic were critical motivators for adopting VE in GJC projects (Askari et al., 2022; Bowen et al., 2019).

The dimensions of virtual exchange and global journalism collaborations

VE projects can be structured in various ways to ensure that their dimensions meet the desired learning outcomes of the subject matter. They involve collaboration between multiple international partners, with some projects involving upwards of six to eight partner universities (Middleweek et al., 2020; Albeanu, 2016). For example, the Global e-News Immersion Initiative is a collaboration between six universities from Chennai, Beirut, Fresno, Coventry, Milwaukee and Stuttgart (Chapter 6). The projects are led by faculty members from each university who oversee their students' work and provide guidance and feedback throughout the learning process.

Student participation in these projects can range from modest groups of 35–60 (Sierra et al., 2022; Bowen et al., 2019; McCullough et al., 2019) to extensive networks involving thousands of students from dozens of universities. For example, Taras et al. (2013) outlines a project that included more than "6000 students from nearly 80 universities located in 43 countries" (p. 163).

It is common for students from partner universities to have similar educational backgrounds. However, having students collaborate with partners who study different but complementary subjects can help them gain experience "working with people with different views, skills and perceptions" (Sierra et al., 2022).

Further, some projects move beyond interdisciplinarity and emphasize the diversity of socioeconomic status among students (Bowen et al., 2019; Bowen et al., 2021; McCullough et al., 2019). For example, a project outlined by Bowen et al. (2019) involves a collaboration between students from a high-income country and students from a low-income country living in a conflict zone. As a result, students received first-hand accounts of cultures and experiences unlike their own (Bowen et al., 2019).

VE projects typically run for four to twelve weeks (Hilliker & Loranc, 2021; Sierra et al., 2022; O'Dowd, 2021; Bowen et al., 2019), with some extending up to a year (McCullough et al., 2019). While tasks and milestones differ, projects usually begin with a written agreement delineating roles and responsibilities (Ferreira-Lopes et al., 2021; McCullough et al., 2019; Anderson et al., 2014). These agreements can be student group contracts, as was the case with Ferreira-Lopes et al. (2021), or broader charters for collaboration (Anderson et al., 2014) and memoranda of understanding between institutions (McCullough et al., 2019). Regardless of the type of agreement, it is crucial to begin VE projects with clearly defined responsibilities for each member (Anderson et al., 2014; Haythornthwaite, 2006).

Initial project meetings foster collaboration by acquainting students and staff with one another through introductions or icebreaker activities (Bowen et al., 2021; Ferreira-Lopes et al., 2021; McCullough et al., 2019). Integrating online lectures and discussions early on in the project also helps prepare students for their collaborative work (Bowen et al., 2021).

All projects culminate in a final collaborative assignment. The nature of these assignments varies based on the subject of study on which the program focuses. For example, projects range from podcasts (Askari et al., 2022), video productions (Antonopoulou, 2019) and news articles (Middleweek et al., 2020; Albeanu, 2016) to presentations (Sierra et al., 2022; McCullough et al., 2019), online forums (Higgins et al., 2013), case studies (Ferreira-Lopes et al., 2021) and analyses (Kolm et al., 2022). Regardless of the nature of the final assignment, Ferreira-Lopes emphasizes that "the idea is to give students a task which demands them to collaborate to deliver a product together" (2021, n.p.).

Within global journalism collaborative projects, it was common for students to act as fixers and report on issues relevant to their partner's country (Bowen et al., 2019; Albeanu, 2016). Projects that pertained to other industries, such as biomedical engineering and global health, followed a similar format. For example, McCullough et al. (2019) outline a project in which students worked to design biomedical products that met the resource needs and restrictions of their partner's country.

Meanwhile, a project explored by Bowen et al. between students in Lebanon and the U.S. had global health students work together to address problems faced by "refugees at a site in the Beqaa Valley in Lebanon" (2021). Upon completing the final assignment, students often participate in a reflection exercise (Taras et al., 2013; Middleweek et al., 2020; Ferreira-Lopes et al., 2021). This allows them to reflect upon the intercultural experience and reinforces learning (Blostein, 2020; Ferreira-Lopes et al., 2021).

Throughout the project process, students communicate using a wide range of tools. While some courses do have students working together with international partners during scheduled class time, students are still required to meet to work on projects outside of class (Hilliker & Loranc, 2021; O'Dowd, 2021; McCullough et al., 2019; Middleweek et al., 2020). These meetings often occur over video conferencing software such as Zoom or Skype (Albeanu, 2016; McCullough et al., 2019; Liu & Shirley, 2021).

Other asynchronous communications through text-based web services like email, Facebook, Slack, WhatsApp, WeChat and other social media platforms are also encouraged and frequently used to maintain communication (O'Dowd, 2021; Bowen et al., 2019; McCullough et al., 2019). In some cases, text-based communication is preferred as it eases the stress of communication for students who are working in a second language (Middleweek et al., 2020).

Throughout the project process, students usually have access to the same resources, which they find through proprietary learning management systems (LMSs) such as the Stanford Online Platform in the case of Bowen et al. (2019) or widely available LMSs such as Google Classroom (Ferreira-Lopes et al., 2021). In the case of a project discussed by Higgins et al. (2013), instructors facilitated the entire project through an online discussion board called ValuePulse (p. 40).

Challenges associated with virtual exchange and global journalism collaboration

The dimensions of VE, while flexible and widely adaptable, present some common challenges. The complexity of international projects requires a great deal of logistical planning, communication and time management (Sierra et al., 2022; Ferreira-Lopes et al., 2021). Scheduling meetings, for example, requires students to contend with differences in time zones (Antonopoulou, 2019; Liu & Shirley, 2021; Taras et al., 2013). Moreover, even when two partner countries are in the same time zone, holidays and semester breaks tend to differ from institution to institution and country to country (Ferreira-Lopes et al., 2021; McCullough et al., 2019).

Ferreira-Lopes et al. (2021) note that a project between universities in Spain and the Netherlands had to accommodate a two-week semester break the Dutch students were provided but the Spanish students were not. The time commitment required from international collaborations can ultimately make it challenging to work these projects into semester timetables (O'Dowd, 2021; McCullough et al., 2019). These logistical challenges also result in a need for greater support from teachers (O'Dowd, 2021; Ferreira-Lopes et al., 2021).

Logistical challenges can be further exacerbated by poor collaboration and communication skills on the part of students. Kolm et al. (2022) identify a skills gap among students, noting that many lack the appropriate international online collaboration competencies (IOCCs) to work in collaborative, online environments. This evaluation is further supported throughout the literature. In particular, students were found to experience difficulties with communication, planning and collaboration (Sierra et al., 2022; O'Dowd, 2021; Middleweek et al., 2020; Kolm et al., 2022). They experienced "different levels of commitment and engagement among group members, asymmetric participation," (Sierra et al., 2022), and overestimated their abilities to use ICTs (Kolm et al., 2022).

Projects like the one discussed by Sierra et al. (2022) involved students participating in online collaboration for the first time. As a result, they noted challenges with the IOCCs mentioned above (Sierra et al., 2022). In contrast, Hilliker and Loranc (2022) outline a project that involved students who had already taken part in a VE. Not surprisingly, these students were more comfortable with online collaboration competencies (Hilliker & Loranc, 2022). Deficits in IOCCs can be regarded as further motivation for adopting online international collaboration into curricula.

In some cases, challenges with communication and collaboration are not the result of a lack of competencies. Instead, they may stem from cultural and professional differences in communication styles (Bowen et al., 2019; Middleweek et al., 2020; Liu & Shirley, 2021; Taras et al., 2013). For example, students from a project outlined by Middleweek et al. (2020) discussed the differences in communication styles between Australian and Ugandan students. Australian students preferred communication through text and email, whereas Ugandan students preferred direct communication through phone calls (Middleweek et al., 2020). These differences in communication style could lead to ill will or frustrations (Bowen et al., 2019).

Furthermore, communication challenges also extend to language barriers (Bowen et al., 2019; Antonopoulou, 2019; Middleweek et al., 2020). GJC projects, such as those discussed by Bowen et al. (2019) and Middleweek et al. (2020), were conducted in English for practical reasons. While project partners in Uganda, Kenya and Pakistan spoke English as a second language, they lacked fluency (Bowen et al., 2019; Middleweek et al., 2020). These language barriers can contribute to inequities among partners since the disparity in English fluency naturally favours native English speakers (Bowen et al., 2019).

Challenges posed by cultural differences further support the need for VE and the importance of critical reflection on intercultural exchange. However, reflection exercises must include close pedagogical monitoring to avoid "the illusion of commonality" (Ware & Kramsch, 2005, as cited in O'Dowd, 2021, n.p.). This term refers to a tendency on the part of students to "minimize cultural differences and reduce [them] to superficial aspects" (O'Dowd, 2021, p. 9). In the case of GJCs, avoiding the illusion of commonality may mean ensuring that students' work is focused on more complex issues, such as politics, education and developmental issues, as opposed to tourism and travel (Bowen et al., 2019).

Developing equitable partnerships also means addressing the challenges associated with digital inequality. As discussed, various projects involved partners from both high-income and low-income countries. Multiple papers call attention to the disparity in the availability and quality of ICTs among partner universities (Bowen et al., 2019; Middleweek et al., 2020; McCullough et al., 2019; Taras et al., 2013). Everything from a lack of affordable broadband and internet service (Middleweek et al., 2020) to sporadic internet connections (Bowen et al., 2019) and available funding for infrastructure (McCullough et al., 2019) could exacerbate communication barriers. Lastly, VE is limited in its ability to allow for complete cultural immersion, allowing only for a simulation of experiences (Bowen et al., 2019).

Student sentiments towards virtual exchange and global journalism collaboration

Despite the challenges and complexity of VE, student sentiments towards these internationalization strategies tend to be largely positive (Liu & Shirley, 2021; McCullough et al., 2019). Moreover, studies by Higgins et al. (2013),

Bowen et al. (2019) and Sierra et al. (2022) all note that engaging in a VE project increased students' interest in the course and its subject matter. Bowen et al. (2019) found that the close relationships students built with their international partners acted as motivation for increased effort.

VE also leads to a greater interest in alternative career paths, such as inspiring students to "pursue a career as a foreign correspondent" (Middleweek et al., 2020) or working on global health initiatives (McCullough et al., 2019). Students felt that they gained more comprehensive interpersonal skills, collaboration (Middleweek et al., 2020) and technical competencies needed in the workplace (O'Dowd, 2021; Hilliker & Loranc, 2021; Liu & Shirley, 2021). In the case of interdisciplinary collaborations, students felt that VE helped them gain skills not addressed by their degree of study (Sierra et al., 2022). However, the most prominent area of skills development is in intercultural sensitivity and collaboration (Ferreira-Lopes et al., 2021; Liu & Shirley, 2021).

Through VE, students gain exposure to inequities between countries, different cultural perspectives on sensitive issues (Liu & Shirley, 2021) and an understanding of how their industry of interest differs in their partner countries (Middleweek et al., 2020). For example, Middleweek et al. (2020) discuss an interaction between two journalism students, one from Australia and one from Uganda:

> We were telling our collaborators that we all want to pursue a career in journalism after Uni, but then when we asked them, they said no. We found this confusing but they soon explained that to be a journalist in Uganda is very risky and dangerous, due to the threat of violence and fear from the current government. So, not only did we all help and benefit from each other in working on our stories, but we also gathered a greater understanding on what journalism really is and how it can be so different and impactful around the world.
>
> (p. 7)

Through online international experiences such as VE, students can expand their understanding of the world and seek new perspectives. They are given a unique opportunity to step out of their comfort zone and learn in an environment built on mutual collaboration. Although VE has its challenges, its potential to positively influence students is great, preparing them for a world as diverse and challenging as the online learning environments that VE enables.

References

Adapa, P. K. (2013). *Strategies and factors effecting internationalization of university research and education*. University of Saskatchewan. Retrieved from https://researchers.usask.ca/phani-adapa/documents/Internationalization.pdf

Albeanu, C. (2016). The GENII Project encourages student journalists from six countries to collaborate on stories. *Journalism.co.uk*. Retrieved from https://www.journalism.co.uk/news/the-genii-project-encourages-student-journalists-from-six-countries-to-collaborate-on-stories/s2/a694832/

Anderson, F., Donkor, P., de Vries, R., Appiah-Denkyira, E., Dakpallah, G. F., Rominski, S., & Ayettey, S. (2014). Creating a charter of collaboration for international university partnerships: The Elmina Declaration for human resources for health. *Academic Medicine: Journal of the Association of American Medical Colleges, 89*(8), 1125–1132. doi:10.1097/ACM.0000000000000384

Antonopoulou, A. (2019). Interdisciplinary collaboration; Narrative and playfulness as a method for civic collaboration and independent learning in higher education. *Liquidificando Dinâmicas de Poder com uma Aprendizagem Híbrida, 4 April 2019, Department of Social Communication, University of Espirito Santo*. Retrieved from https://ualresearchonline.arts.ac.uk/id/eprint/16417

Askari, A., Meechan, P., Ruiz-Rodríguez, P., & Torres Sánchez, S. (2022). Virtual exchange course fosters "global competency" for student journalists. *Society of Environmental Journalists*. Retrieved from https://www.sej.org/publications/ej-academy/virtual-exchange-course-fosters-global-competency-student-journalists

Blostein, S. (2020). *Tips for virtual exchange and engaging partners online*. Guelph, ON: University of Guelph. https://atrium.lib.uoguelph.ca/xmlui/handle/10214/2501

Bowen, K., Barry, M., Jowell, A., Maddah, D., & Alami, N. H. (2021). Virtual exchange in global health: An innovative educational approach to foster socially responsible overseas collaboration. *International Journal of Educational Technology in Higher Education, 18*(1), 32–32. doi:10.1186/s41239-021-00266-x

Bowen, K., Ullah Khan, A., & Wake, A. (2019). Virtual student exchange in journalism: Collaborative reporting through new media and technology. *Australian Journalism Review, 41*(1), 53–66. doi:10.1386/ajr.41.1.53_1

Ferreira-Lopes, L., Elexpuru-Albizuri, I., & Bezanilla, M. J. (2021). Developing business students' intercultural competence through intercultural virtual collaboration: A task sequence implementation. *Journal of International Education in Business, 14*(2), 338–360. doi:10.1108/JIEB-06-2020-0055

Haythornthwaite, C. (2006). Facilitating collaboration in online learning. *Journal of Asynchronous Learning Networks, 10*(1), 7–24. doi:10.24059/olj.v10i1.1769

Hénard, F., Diamond, L., & Roseveare, D. (2012). Approaches to internationalization and their implications for strategic management and institutional practice: A guide for higher education institutions. *OECD*. Retrieved from https://www.oecd.org/education/imhe/Approaches%20to%20internationalization%20-%20final%20-%20web.pdf

Higgins, L., Wolf, M. M. G., & Torres, A. M. (2013). Opening the doors to a global classroom: An international social media collaboration. *NACTA Journal, 57*(3a), 40–44. Retrieved from http://www.jstor.org/stable/nactajournal.57.3a.40

Hilliker, S. M., & Loranc, B. (2022). Development of 21st century skills through virtual exchange. *Teaching and Teacher Education, 112*, 1–8. doi:10.1016/j.tate.2022.103646

Kolm, A., de Nooijer, J., Vanherle, K., Werkman, A., Wewerka-Kreimel, D., Rachman-Elbaum, S., & van Merriënboer, J. J. G. (2022). International online collaboration competencies in higher education students: A systematic review. *Journal of Studies in International Education, 26*(2), 183–201.

Liu, Y., & Shirley, T. (2021). Without crossing a border: Exploring the impact of shifting study abroad online on students' learning and intercultural competence development during the COVID-19 pandemic. *Online Learning (Newburyport, Mass.)*, *25*(1), 182. doi:10.24059/olj.v25i1.2471

Marinoni, G. (2019). *Internationalization of higher education: An evolving landscape, locally and globally: IAU 5th global survey*. Deutsche Universitätszeitung: Berlin Academic Publishers. Retrieved from https://www.google.com/url?q=https://www.iau-aiu.net/IMG/pdf/iau_5th_global_survey_executive_summary.pdf&sa=D&source=docs&ust=1689691285658299&usg=AOvVaw0Rr4ud0OmUZD2VbZVAGIkK

McCullough, M., Msafiri, N., Richardson, W. J., Harman, M. K., DesJardins, J. D., & Dean, D. (2019). Development of a global design education experience in bioengineering through international partnerships. *Journal of Biomechanical Engineering*, *141*(12), 1–8. doi:10.1115/1.4045112

Middleweek, B., Mutsvairo, B., & Attard, M. (2020). Toward a theorization of student journalism collaboration in international curricula. *Journalism & Mass Communication Educator*, *75*(4), 407–418. doi:10.1177/1077695820922725

O'Dowd, R. (2021). What do students learn in virtual exchange? A qualitative content analysis of learning outcomes across multiple exchanges. *International Journal of Educational Research*, *109*, 1–13. doi:10.1016/j.ijer.2021.101804.

Sierra, J., Yassim, M., & Suárez-Collado, Á. (2022). Together we can: Enhancing key 21st-century skills with international virtual exchange. *Education & Training*, *64*(6), 826–843. doi:10.1108/ET-05-2021-0171

Taras, V., Caprar, D. V., Rottig, D., Sarala, R. M., Zakaria, N., Zhao, F., & Huang, V. Z. (2013). A global classroom? Evaluating the effectiveness of global virtual collaboration as a teaching tool in management education. *Academy of Management Learning & Education*, *12*(3), 414–435.

2 Student engagement
How the Global News Relay began

Sarah Jones

Figure 2.1

In July 2013, 330 participants from 55 countries gathered at the World Journalism Education Congress (WJEC) in Mechelen, Belgium. Panels, seminars and plenaries all focused on what skills journalism students needed going into a digital-first news industry. Surrounded by educators, all with shared challenges, a simple thought crossed my mind,

what if we all came together, with our students, and worked collaboratively? That thought is what became the Global News Relay.

The global news relay: the idea

The news industry in 2013 was fast responding to the challenges of digital and social media, coupled with a decline in newspaper readership. The UK's communications regulator, Ofcom's News Consumption in the UK report (2013) found that 78% of adults used television as their source for news, with 40% using newspapers. Almost a third sourced their news from the internet (Ofcom, 2013). At this time, the television rolling news channels (24-hour, continuously updated coverage) were an "increasingly inescapable part of the contemporary landscape" (Cushion & Lewis, 2010, p. 1).

DOI: 10.4324/9781003428725-3

The rise in rolling news and increases in digital consumption had a significant impact on journalism culture and practice. Saltzis (2012) argued that the change in time blurs established news formats, focusing on a continuum instead of working to a fixed deadline. This changes the nature of newsgathering, and how it is compiled, constructed and consumed (Brighton & Foy, 2007, p. 41). Theorists have pointed to this as evolving to a fluid news cycle (Saltzis, 2012) with the impact continuing to influence the culture of journalism and the news industry (Cushion & Lewis, 2010).

The concept of a rolling news channel fuelled the initial idea of the Global News Relay. Instead of a news channel, broadcasting content for 24 hours a day, universities would work collaboratively and do the same. Twenty-four universities could each produce one hour of content, moving each hour to the next university in the next country, effectively passing a virtual relay baton. At that time it was ambitious as a project. Journalism programmes in universities did not usually broadcast externally. Broadcasts are usually part of news days and the longest tend to be around 20 minutes duration. This would require a significant amount of resources from staff and the universities, and engagement and commitment from students.

Networks formed at the WJEC provided the initial partners. Institutional partners at people's universities provided further collaborators. Each thought about different ways that they could be part of a rolling news platform for journalism students across the world. Despite the challenges that were inevitable involving technology, university structures, different time zones and even academic calendars, all were committed to the ambition that we had an opportunity to increase global competencies amongst our students, best preparing them for journalistic careers.

The global news relay: the rationale

The COVID-19 pandemic has provided many lessons for different ways of working and studying through technology with many citing changes in multiple, complex and overlapping needs (Kamarianos et al., 2020). In 2013, complex collaborations were just starting to form, and the term virtual mobility was emerging.

The university sector had begun to place increasing emphasis on internationalisation of the curriculum and of teaching and learning. Mobility was a focus, and de Wit (2017) argued for virtual mobility. Physical mobility was increasing with more students taking up opportunities for study abroad or international field trips, but this meant a large number of students were excluded for socio-economic reasons. For de Wit, virtual mobility focuses on the "'internationalisation at home' movement" (2017, p. 83) and conceptualising projects that would "make it possible for non-mobile students to develop an international dimension to their teaching and learning" (2013, p. 83).

Collaborative Online International Learning (COIL) was the answer to virtual mobility. These are projects that bring about collaboration between staff and students at different institutions. They use technology in design and utilise online interactions. They have international dimensions, in terms of the project scope and design or the nature of the collaborations, and they are integrated into the pedagogical design of a programme. An example of a COIL, given by de Wit in 2017, was from the Amsterdam University of Applied Sciences and partner universities in Paris and Barcelona. The students worked on real-life projects in the three cities, beginning with a one-week visit to Amsterdam. They worked collaboratively online in the weeks that followed, tackling the issues of the live brief that had been sent. In the final week, the students came together once more, to present work and discuss results. They were interacting in both the virtual and physical sense.

The European Commission was starting to use the term virtual mobility, to capture activities like the one above, where critical intercultural competencies were being developed. Research has found increases in many learner skills from those partaking in COILs and virtual mobility projects, including networked learning, media and digital literacies, autonomy-driven learning and open-mindedness (Rajagopal et al., 2020). An Erasmus report (European Commission, 2018) found 64% of employers said international experiences in a candidate were extremely desirable, arguing that these candidates had a unique skillset and different experiences to share. The employability of students with global competencies and experience is well documented.

> Multinational employers, and increasingly employers of all kinds, require their workforce to work readily and confidently across worldwide operations, using a global outlook to consider new opportunities and challenges.
> (Diamond et al., 2011, p. 5)

For many students, the idea of being able to afford the time and the expense of travelling overseas, completing a global experience or work placements internationally is not possible. Students have increasingly complex lives and

COIL project	Global news relay
A collaborative exercise of teachers and students.	Teams of staff and students. Collaboration both within the institution and between other institutions.
Makes use of online technology and interaction.	Different platforms were used for preparation, editorial meetings and collaborations. These ranged from social networks to video conference calls.
It has potential international dimensions.	By collaborating with many institutions in different countries, students are exposed to different cultures and develop awareness of news practices and the news values in different places.
It is integrated into the learning process.	Run within modules, where possible.

responsibilities so such experiences can be prohibitive. COILs and virtual mobility open these opportunities to a more diverse group of students.

With this rationale, the Global News Relay developed to fully align with de Wit's definition of a COIL.

The latter is the most challenging, as anyone working in universities will be aware of. Each institution operates their own calendars, module structures and credit values. It has not been possible to align this for all involved. Instead, it has had to be adapted to suit each institutions' own practices for assessment.

The critical factor in developing the Global News Relay was to internationalise the curriculum and allow for global experiences to support our students, affording new opportunities. Many university strategies will include reference to this, and the Global News Relay defined how it can embed internationalisation into teaching and learning to reach successful outcomes.

The global news relay: the reality

The original intent was to broadcast for 24 hours in 24 different locations. Technical capability and people's capacity meant this over ambitious plan was rethought. Instead, the University of Salford as the lead institution, collaborated with ten institutions, each tasked with producing an hour of content. This meant that the precedent set by rolling news organisations of repeat scheduling would occur at selected intervals during the broadcast.

The decision was made to broadcast via YouTube on a website that was public facing, and the programme would be streamed live. The live passing of the baton was not achievable with the limited technical capabilities, so instead, content was transferred and played out from the lead institution's studio. To meet the objectives that we would collaboratively produce a coherent global news programme, it was decided that the weather would provide a natural link between segments. This is an example of the link between the University of Salford in the UK and the Asian College of Journalism in Chennai, India:

> The South Coast will see the best weather with sun throughout the day, highs of eight degrees, but it'll feel a lot cooler in the wind. So now we're off to India next where the weather is a lot different to ours. There are no signs of showers across the country and temperatures are in their high thirties. So now we'll pass over to the Asian College of Journalism in Chennai where it's a very warm 35 degrees.
>
> (Quays News, 2014)

As with any broadcast, there were technical challenges meaning that students had to think quickly, be responsive and agile, all of which are crucial transferable skills for future employability. A red holding screen saying, resumes shortly, allowed the students to cue the right programmes and gather themselves. One programme was broadcast without sound, which meant that a presenter in the studio had to ad lib, apologise and manage the output:

18 *Sarah Jones*

> Sorry about the technical issues there with India. We will be returning to them in the programme, but now here's our colleagues from Dubai.
>
> (Global News Relay, 2014)

Research within journalism education has supported the value of simulated and experiential learning environments with many students reporting a deeper learning experience from being in a real media environment and just "doing it for real" (Steel et al., 2007, p. 330). This is becoming increasingly more important as the industry relies more on freelancers and news organisations face redundancies leaving fewer opportunities for real-world learning experiences (Valencia-Forrester, 2020).

The Global News Relay provided that level of simulated learning and real-world experience, intensified by working collaboratively with students from across the world, which they would not have had otherwise. This developed global competencies and awareness of the international news agenda in a unique learning experience.

The global news relay: the impact

In the first year, hundreds of students took part in the Global News Relay generating news coverage in industry press (Bartlett, 2014), recognising the ambition of such a collaborative project.

Students worked collaboratively across borders, learning about different news agendas, how news is reported and style choices including pieces to camera, set design and graphics. Editorial meetings took place and allowed students to talk about what stories they would be covering and this provided one of the key learnings from the project.

Dan was a second-year student who was passionate about learning and loved news. He was the first in his family to attend university and had never travelled far from his hometown. During the weeks leading up to the Global News Relay, he ran in, full of excitement and said he couldn't believe that he was just in an editorial meeting in India. This is the transformational notion of international collaborations for students.

It was important to draw on the online and technological aspects of de Wit's COIL projects, whilst enabling students to develop digital literacies that could help them in a future-facing newsroom. A small team looked at experimenting with new platforms, including TV Interact. This pulled in content from social platforms which were then developed into a graphic sequence for broadcast. Utilising new technologies, helped students to get early insight into the integration of social media and second screen viewing, which were skills they could then develop in follow-on assignments.

The Global News Relay has had a significant impact on student engagement and enhancing their educational experience. It has become a vehicle for virtual mobility and a COIL project to ensure that students are global in their outlook. Personal feedback submitted by staff at other institutions evidences the impact that this has had.

Devadas Rajaram, Asian College of Journalism, Chennai, India

Global News Relay (GNR) has broadened the understanding of my students, providing them diverse perspectives on issues around the world. It's truly been a unique learning experience, in terms of widening their reach and instilled more confidence in them. The collaborative nature of the project has been an immensely useful opportunity for my students to widen their peer network and participation in GNR has enabled them to look for and gain more employment and opportunities elsewhere.

(Personal communication, 2015)

The impact that the Global News Relay has had on employability of students is a similar finding at Manipal University in Dubai, supporting the evidence of the Erasmus report (2018) that employers seek students who have developed global competencies and international experiences.

Sabir Haque, Manipal University, Dubai

The concept of the Global News Relay, which can bring together under one platform, news stories from across the world is a noble one. My students benefited by comparing their work with students across the world. Although the news gathering environment may be remarkably different from one city to another, nevertheless, working within the limitations or lack of any, opens up opportunities, which was the main takeaway for the students.

(Personal communication, 2015)

Concluding thoughts

The Global News Relay met the objectives of students around the world, collaborating and producing news together. It has proved a model for changing educators' perspectives and impacting others as well as transforming students.

It has provided a snapshot of journalism across the world, told by the students who would later become reporters, presenters, and editors in broadcasting companies globally. The students developed an understanding of the global news agenda and built networks of peers and contacts all over the world. They had a real-world environment to work in, which although it drew in a global audience and received international press coverage, it provided a safe space to test ideas involving new technologies and different ways of reporting the news.

Most importantly, the students who were involved were highly engaged in the work, not wishing to let their teams down, but also knowing that students all over were watching and taking part too. They gained confidence in their abilities and their potential to work as international journalists. It is perhaps no surprise that many went on to work as journalists in many global news outlets.

References

Bartlett, R. (2014). Students across world take part in Global News Relay. *Journalism News*. Retrieved from https://www.journalism.co.uk/news/students-across-world-take-part-in-global-news-relay/s2/a556249/

Brighton, P., & Foy, D. (2007). *News values*. Sage, London. doi:10.4135/9781446216026

Cushion, S., & Lewis, J. (Ed.) (2010). *The rise of 24-hour news television: Global perspectives*. Peter Lang: New York.

de Wit, H. (2017). Global: Coil—Virtual mobility without commercialisation. *University World News, Understanding Higher Education Internationalization*, 1 June 2013, *274*, 83–85.

Diamond, A., Walkley, L., Forbes, P., Hughes, T., & Sheen, J. (2011). *Global graduates into global leaders*. Paper presented by The Association of Graduate Recruiters, The Council for Industry and Higher Education and CFE Research and Consulting, London. Retrieved from https://www.ncub.co.uk/wp-content/uploads/2011/06/CIHE-1111GlobalGradsFull.pdf

European Commission, Directorate-General for Education, Youth, Sport and Culture. (2018). *Combined evaluation of Erasmus+ and predecessor programmes: Executive summary*. Publications Office. doi:10.2766/45042

Kamarianos, I., Adamopoulou, A., Lambropoulos, H., & Stamelos, G. (2020). Towards an understanding of university students' response in times of pandemic crisis (Covid-19). *European Journal of Education Studies*, *7*(7), 20–39.

Ofcom (2013a) Communications Market Report 2013. London: Ofcom. Retrieved from: https://www.ofcom.org.uk/__data/assets/pdf_file/0021/19731/2013_uk_cmr.pdf

Quays News. (2014). *Global news relay 2014*. Retrieved from https://youtube/_Qw6Xgor71E

Rajagopal, K., Firssova, O., de Beeck, I. O., Van der Stappen, E., Stoyanov, S., Henderikx, P., & Buchem, I. (2020). Learner skills in open virtual mobility. *Research in Learning Technology*, *28*, 1–18. doi:10.25304/rlt.v28.2254

Saltzis, K. (2012). Breaking news online: How news stories are updated and maintained around-the-clock. *Journalism Practice*, *6*(5–6), 702–710. doi:10.1177/1464884916689151

Steel, J., Carmichael, B., Holmes, D., Kinse, M., & Sanders, K. (2007). Experiential learning and journalism education: Lessons learned in the practice of teaching journalism. *Education+ Training*, *49*(4), 325–334.

Valencia-Forrester, F. (2020). Models of work-integrated learning in journalism education. *Journalism Studies*, *21*(5), 697–712.

3 Global News Relay (GNR) 2.0

Faith Sidlow and Katherine C. Blair

Figure 3.1 Global News Relay Control Room in Fresno, Calif., U.S.

Shortly after the first iteration of the Global News Relay in March 2014, Professor Sarah Jones spoke by Skype at a global collaboration panel session at the Excellence in Journalism conference in Nashville, Tennessee. The panel was moderated by Dr. Butler Cain from West Texas A&M, whose students participated in Jones' first Global News Relay.

Three other professors attended that panel—from California State University, Fresno, University of Alabama and Baylor University in Texas. All three signed on for the next Global News Relay project planned for March 2015. The goal was a 24-hour global newscast with 24 universities.

The organizers at Salford contacted faculty at the other universities in January to say plans had changed. Jones was leaving Salford at the end of February, and they wanted to do a smaller program before her departure. They decided to center the stories around the theme of poverty and condense the show from 24 hours to two hours. Ten universities signed on including Fresno State.

DOI: 10.4324/9781003428725-4

With only one month to plan, produce and stream, faculty and students were presented with a new set of challenges and opportunities. Students at Fresno State had just started their term. Many had never shot or edited a news story. They agreed to try and came up with six different stories related to the poverty theme: homelessness, hunger, the California drought, the Fresno State Student Cupboard (food pantry), Fresno M.E.A.L (Meals Engaging All Lives), a homeless shelter and the plight of valley farmers (Sidlow, 2015).

The stories produced during the 2015 GNR left a profound impact on participating students, transcending borders and shaping their future careers.

Angelica Leilani, a Fresno State student who reported on a group of people who prepared lunches for the homeless, said she was able to take what she learned from the Global News Relay and apply it to her first two reporting jobs after she graduated.

Angelica Leilani, Fresno State broadcast journalism major and former TV news reporter

> At that point in my life I had never been out of the country, and so to connect with the other students and the different aspects that they put into their stories and see how it all flowed together was really exciting. It gave me the confidence I needed to get my first TV job in a small market and then move up to a larger market.
>
> (Personal communication, July 27, 2023)

In the end, Leilani won a California State University Media Arts Festival Award for her GNR story and another Fresno State student won an Associated Press award for Best Feature Story. Students' participation in the GNR also led to a $26,000 grant to buy new production equipment, which would allow Fresno State to begin hosting the Global News Relay the following year.

Go to this link to view the entire two-hour and 20-minute program from 2015 hosted by students at Salford University: bit.ly/Ch3GNR15. (Quays TV, 2015).

The concept

The evolution of the global news relay

When Fresno State took over hosting duties in 2016, the goal was to fulfill Sarah Jones' original vision of 24 universities broadcasting 24 hours of international news based on a common, newsworthy theme. Dozens of universities were contacted, but only 13 committed, and none agreed to produce an hour of content. As a result, the relay was streamlined into a four-and-a-half-hour production, but the spirit of collaboration remained unwavering.

24 *Faith Sidlow and Katherine C. Blair*

The 2016 theme: the impact of sports in your community

Several of the instructors who were involved in the 2015 iteration met in person at the Excellence in Journalism conference in Orlando, Florida that year to plan the 2016 program. A professor from Texas State University proposed the theme of the "impact of sports in your community" to coincide with the 2016 Summer Olympics in Brazil. The idea was to get students to explore how sports transcends athletic programs and becomes an integral part of community life. The theme delved into health and obesity issues, community engagement and the impact of injuries related to sports (Castañon, 2016)

Fresno State hosted the production with its students producing and anchoring the entire program. Each participating university created pre-produced 15-to-20-minute newscasts. Collaborative efforts were facilitated through various communication channels such as Google Hangouts, Facebook chat, Skype video meetings and emails. Student producers checked in with the coordinators from each university to answer questions and make sure deadlines were being met.

The final program was then broadcast live on a local public access channel and YouTube. Go to this link to view the 2016 GNR: bit.ly/Ch3GNR16. (CMAC, 2016).

The process

The Global News Relay (GNR) process requires a well-coordinated effort that involves universities worldwide coming together to produce 15-to-20-minute newscasts on a common theme. It requires all participants to commit, communicate and meet deadlines.

Planning starts in November for the following spring semester. A core group of instructors collaboratively decides on a theme that will unite all participating universities in their storytelling endeavors. To ensure widespread participation, the host university reaches out to journalism and media instructors at universities that have previously taken part or expressed an interest in joining the GNR.

Effective communication is important for the success of the GNR. At the start of the spring semester, coordinators and students from the participating universities connect by video conferencing platforms such as Zoom, Google Meet, Microsoft Teams or WhatsApp to explain the process and answer questions.

To streamline communication and ensure deadlines are met, student coordinators from the host university are assigned to each participating university. These coordinators serve as liaisons, facilitating exchanges between the participating institutions allowing students to fully immerse themselves in the planning process and ensuring ample time for content creation.

To encourage interaction and collaboration between students and faculty from partner universities, social media groups are established on Facebook,

Slack or WhatsApp. These platforms provide a space for participants to share ideas, discuss progress and foster a sense of camaraderie.

To maintain technical consistency, a one-sheet prep document is provided to all universities. This document outlines technical and communication specifications ensuring a cohesive production.

A well-crafted social media plan is developed to promote the upcoming GNR. Logos from each participating university are collected to create a banner for use on social media and the GNR website. Additionally, teasers or promos showcasing the students' stories are collected and shared on social media to generate excitement.

To highlight the uniqueness and accomplishments of each university, institutional ads promoting their departments or programs are collected and featured during the broadcast.

A Google Drive folder is created to serve as a centralized repository for universities to upload their assets, including promos, ads and video stories.

Creating a seamless global newscast involves meticulous scheduling based on time zones. We use the virtual time converter (worldtimebuddy.com) to determine the time zones and schedule each university. The production team builds the GNR with graphic openers, music, lower thirds (on-screen name and title captions) and end credits. Lower third templates are shared with the participating universities to give the GNR a consistent look. During the live broadcast, pre-produced videos from each university are incorporated, followed by Skype or Zoom talkbacks with each anchor team.

Although the first several iterations of the Global News Relay were broadcast live with a student director and technical director taking the video packages live, the more recent versions were recorded with video packages inserted in post-production allowing for a cleaner product.

The Global News Relay themes from 2014 to 2023 are listed below:

2014 General news
2015 Poverty
2016 Sports in your community
2017 Solutions journalism
2018 Homelessness
2019 Migration
2020 Voices of Gen Z in climate change
2021 How COVID changed us
2022 Mind matters
2023 Global supply chain

Challenges

The spring of 2020 brought unprecedented challenges because of the COVID-19 pandemic. Hong Kong Baptist University, the host school that year, was locked out of their studio because of COVID restrictions, forcing students to produce stories and anchor shows from their bedrooms. Despite the challenges, the spirit of collaboration prevailed, enabling the GNR to adapt and persevere.

As the world started to return to a new normal following two years of the pandemic, the effect on people's mental health was evident. To reflect this reality, the topic of mental health was chosen for the 2022 theme.

Mind Matters was to be hosted from HKBU once again, and efforts started to gather participants in late 2021. But when Hong Kong's COVID lockdown tightened its grip, the university faced a dilemma—how could they produce a global television program, linking eight universities across thirteen time zones and five countries all while social distancing under the strictest of conditions? They asked the partner universities for help, and Leeds Trinity University (LTU) in the UK stepped up.

Luckily, a talented cohort of Master of Arts journalism students went into overdrive to make it happen. The students, who weren't being assessed on the project, worked weekends and into their Easter holiday to make the show happen—writing scripts, pulling in programs from the universities and communicating with each university's host, who would do the as-live debriefs after each section.

It was a last-minute task for senior media technician Mark Willett to work out how to put the show together technically. He had already been using StreamYard, a subscription platform LTU adopted for its annual Journalism & Media Week, which brings together industry experts as guest speakers. During the pandemic, this had to be done remotely. It had been successfully used with higher quality video output than Microsoft Teams and acted like a vision mixer as well in allowing graphic overlays and multiple screen setups. It also allowed simultaneous transmission to multiple social media platforms such as Facebook, YouTube and Twitter.

Willett decided this would be a good platform for the GNR. Although gallery talkback was more complicated, he was able to arrange it so students from the other universities could hear LTU's presenters speaking from the studio.

The anchor debriefs or talkbacks were pre-recorded and then edited into the program in post-production. The resulting two-and-a-quarter-hour show demonstrated effective pre- and post-production skills. Student feedback was overwhelmingly positive. Most said they got a lot out of it and honed their production skills and their understanding of bringing a big news program together (Blair, 2022).

It felt even more real than the live daily news programs they had been producing in the two weeks leading up to production as part of their TV newsdays.

You can see the whole program, Global News Relay 2022 Mind Matters, on YouTube at this link: bit.ly/Ch3GNR22 (Global Journalism Collaboration, 2022).

For 2023, the relay was handed back to HKBU, with the theme of the global supply chain. Go to this link to view the 2023 GNR: bit.ly/Ch3GNR23 (Lam, 2023).

Other challenges

Left to themselves, students have not been able to complete the projects. This type of hands-on learning requires a certain level of synergy among professors, instructors, staff and students. Students who are assessed for their work on the GNR typically are more motivated than those who don't receive grades. However, in many cases when clubs or extracurricular groups participate, these students turn out some of the best work. Also, students whose goal is to work in the media industry are more engaged.

Often, students at the host university are intimidated by reaching out to strangers in far-away places. And occasionally cultural differences or poor etiquette can cause offense.

In one example, a Fresno State student wrote a terse email with brief instructions to a professor in the United Arab Emirates without a proper salutation or a "please" or "thank you." After I wrote an apology to the professor, he responded that he was "taken aback" by the student's email.

In another example, a British student was waiting to read his lines during a rehearsal and had his feet propped up on a coffee table, showing the bottoms of his shoes to the camera. To people in India, the Middle East and Asia, that's an insult.

Students from Rafik Hariri University in Beirut were particularly challenged because of a lack of resources but still wanted to take part.

"We had no broadcast facility and no broadcast program," said Sandra Whitehead, a lecturer at the university who recruited her students to participate in the GNR. She said one of the best parts of the experience was the collaboration between the Lebanese students and the students at Fresno State.

Sandra Whitehead, Lecturer, Rafik Hariri University, Beirut

> I'm a print journalist and I taught it from the angle of reporting and writing. We had a fold up table and we were in the auditorium. Your students were so wonderful. They said, OK. We can make this work for you guys. Just do this, and we'll do that. It was great.
>
> (Personal Communication, May 18, 2023)

Communication among the students in the various countries was made more complicated by the inconsistent TV terms. Terms varied even among the different professional networks in the same country. For example, in the U.S., many TV stations used the term VO for a voice over, when the news anchor reads a script with video played over the narration. At some organizations in the UK, it's called an underlay: ULAY/OOV.

The time difference is one of the greatest challenges. When it's 5 p.m. in California, it's 1 a.m. in London and 8 a.m. in China. When producing a live broadcast of 20-minute segments, someone somewhere is going to have to go live in the middle of the night. That makes it impossible to schedule all of the universities at convenient times. Scheduling is further complicated by geographic location in the northern versus southern hemisphere. Many universities below the equator are on opposite academic schedules from their northern counterparts.

Benefits

Still, the benefits far outweigh the challenges.

In 2017, Fresno State hosted the Global News Relay with students at 17 universities creating content around the theme *Solutions Journalism* (Albeanu, 2017). Former Fresno State multimedia student Natalie Nigg worked on the production side of the GNR for three semesters, including the 2017 program. She said she got excited about working with students at all of the other universities.

Natalie Nigg, Former multimedia student, Fresno State

> You're working with someone from a completely different country in a time zone that's 12 hours different than you in a culture that's completely the opposite of yours. I don't know why you wouldn't want to be 110% involved. This is a once in a lifetime experience, and you're not going to be able to do this at this level unless you go work for a big national network.
>
> (Personal Communication, July 16, 2023)

You can see the entire 2017 program on YouTube at this link: bit.ly/Ch3GNR17. (Global News Relay, 2017).

The table below illustrates how the Global News Relay reaches more than just the participating students (Table 3.1).

Table 3.1 2017 Global News Relay in numbers

Impact by the numbers in 2017	
17	Universities
10	Countries
44	Fresno State students
255	Students worldwide
4	Fresno State faculty
51	Faculty worldwide
85	Solutions Journalism themed stories
26,000	Twitter impressions on the airdate
8,500	Live stream views
7	Live Skype interviews
4	Live set interviews
6	Hours on air

In 2018, Fresno State hosted the largest Global News Relay starting with 22 universities (Albeanu, 2018). Two weeks before the air date, three universities dropped out as some instructors didn't understand the expectations. Because students at many of the universities weren't graded or assessed, there wasn't an incentive to produce work, and they missed the deadlines. Then, one day before the live show, a fourth university dropped out, leaving 18. Go to this link bit.ly/Ch3GNR2018 to see the 2018 program (Fresno State Focus TV, 2018).

Nigg said the days leading up to the live show allowed little time for sleep because of all of the production requirements.

Natalie Nigg, Former multimedia student, Fresno State

We built bumpers for the beginning and the end of each university, and we had 18 that year. Plus, we had a whole host of graphics, not to mention the promos. And then I was in charge of making sure that the crew knew where they were supposed to be. It was just so big with so many moving parts. I think it changed my life because that's the most proud I've ever been on a project because it was the longest one. It was pretty seamless for what it was. And it taught me how to work really well under pressure.

(Personal Communication, July 16, 2023)

Jenny Lam, whose university has participated in the Global News Relay for six years and has hosted for four years, said her students benefit by getting exposure to other students around the world.

Jenny Lam, Senior Lecturer, Hong Kong Baptist University

> They don't always have a very global perspective. So connecting with people like themselves, in other words broadcast students in other universities, is a great experience so that they know that other students may or may not be as unaware as they are. So it's really just a place for them to know that we're not alone in this.
>
> (Personal communication, May 26, 2023)

For students at Fresno State, the Global News Relay motivated them to produce outstanding work, and it created a momentum that has continued throughout the semester with students more engaged, working better together as a team and producing award-winning journalism projects (Sidlow, 2015). Ninety percent of the students who participated in the Global News Relay at Fresno State ended up finding jobs in the news industry and used the skills they learned in professional news media jobs.

Over the past decade, the Global News Relay has changed and evolved, bringing in additional universities while others dropped off. Much of the change came as a result of lecturers, instructors and tutors leaving the university where the GNR was produced without being able to persuade another instructor to commit to taking over the reins. However, in a few cases, instructors took the GNR with them to their new university.

The table below shows the evolution of the Global News Relay, from its inception at Salford University with Sarah Jones to its current iteration hosted by Hong Kong Baptist University. The dots indicate the year(s) each university participated (Table 3.2).

The process behind the Global News Relay demonstrates the power of effective planning, communication and collaboration. From early involvement of students and faculty to leveraging social media and technology, the GNR exemplifies how universities worldwide can unite to create an impactful global news experience. The journey continues, fostering lifelong connections and nurturing the next generation of global journalists.

Table 3.2 Global News Relay Participation and Host Universities

		2014	2015	2016	2017	2018	2019	2020	2021	2022	2023
1	Salford University	Host Univ	Host Univ			●	●	●	●		
2	Fresno State		●	Host Univ	Host Univ	Host Univ	●	●			
3	Hong Kong Baptist University					●	Host Univ	Host Univ	Host Univ	●	Host Univ
4	Leeds Trinity University								●	Host Univ	
5	American University in Bulgaria			●	●	●					
6	American University in Cairo		●		●	●					
7	Asian College of Journalism	●	●		●	●	●	●	●	●	●
8	Baylor University			●	●	●		●			
9	Binus University, Jakarta, Indonesia	●			●	●	●	●	●		
10	Boston University			●							
11	Breda University of Applied Sciences NHTV					●	●	●	●		
12	Columbia College, Chicago	●									
13	Communication University of China					●		●		●	●
14	Coventry University		●	●	●	●	●	●	●	●	●
15	Edith Cowan University Perth, Australia	●									
16	Escuela de Periodismo Carlos Septién García				●						
17	Tel Aviv University								●	●	●
18	Kochi University				●	●					
19	London South Bank University					●		●			
20	Macleay College, Sydney Australia		●	●							
21	Manipal University, Dubai	●			●	●	●	●			
22	Marquette University				●						
23	Nanjing University, China				●	●	●				
24	Rafik Hariri University, Beirut				●						
25	RMIT Melbourne, Australia	●									

(Continued)

Table 3.2 (Continued)

		2014	2015	2016	2017	2018	2019	2020	2021	2022	2023
26	Royal Institute for Theatre, Cinema and Sound (RITCS) Brussels								●		
27	Ryerson University					●	●	●			
28	San Francisco State University	●									
29	Tunku Abdul Rahman (TAR) University College Malaysia	●									
30	Texas State University			●	●	●	●	●	●	●	
31	Texas Tech University								●		
32	University of Alabama		●	●	●	●					
33	University of Johannesburg								●		
34	University of North Alabama		●			●		●			
35	University of the West of England			●	●	●			●	●	●
36	Volda University College Norway	●									
37	West Texas A&M	●	●	●							

References

Albeanu, C. (2017). The latest Global News Relay is tackling solutions journalism in 10 countries. *journalism.co.uk*. Retrieved from https://www.journalism.co.uk/podcast/the-latest-global-news-relay-is-tackling-solutions-journalism-in-10-countries/s399/a701874/

Albeanu, C. (2018). 'Shelter' around the world: Students from 22 universities team up for fifth Global News Relay to produce 7 hours of storytelling. *journalism.co.uk*. Retrieved from https://www.journalism.co.uk/news/global-news-relay-shelter/s2/a719629/

Blair, K. (2022). Global TV projects in journalism education. *Journalism Education*, *11*(1), 42–59.

Castañon, E. (2016). Student reporters at Fresno State serve as centerpiece for global news report. *Fresno State Magazine*. Retrieved from https://magazine.fresnostate.edu/a-student-broadcast-heard-round-the-world/

CMAC. (2016). *Global News Relay 2016*. [Video]. YouTube. Retrieved from https://www.youtube.com/watch?v=Tg_e1S9RvjA&ab_channel=CMAC

Fresno State Focus TV. (2018). *Global News Relay 2018- shelter*. [Video]. YouTube. Retrieved from https://www.youtube.com/watch?v=46pCZdcKx7Q&ab_channel=FresnoStateFocusTV

Global Journalism Collaboration. (2022). *Global News Relay 2022: Mind matters*. [Video]. YouTube. Retrieved from

Global News Relay. (2017). *Global News Relay: Solutions journalism - March 29, 2017*. [Video]. YouTube. Retrieved from https://www.youtube.com/watch?v=cI3ibqhXPS0&ab_channel=GlobalNewsRelay

Lam, J. (2023). *Global News Relay 2023*. [Video]. YouTube. Retrieved from https://www.youtube.com/watch?v=L6xDyakUt7s&ab_channel=JennyLam

Quays TV. (2015). *Global News: Poverty 2015*. [Video]. YouTube. Retrieved from https://www.youtube.com/watch?v=-HJ3796zBgY&ab_channel=QuaysTV

Sidlow, F. (2015). *Global News Relay: Poverty world-wide student journalism collaboration* [Poster]. Fresno State. Retrieved from https://adminfinance.fresnostate.edu/orgexcellence/documents/caife/psoepdfs/PSOE%20PP%20Global%20News%20

worldtimebuddy. (n.d.). Retrieved from https://www.worldtimebuddy.com/

4 Global Campus Studio Productions (GCSP)

Marion Coomey

Figure 4.1 Global Campus Studio Productions, Toronto Metropolitan University, Canada.

The concept

The idea for Global Campus Studio Productions (GCSP) originated in 2000. I had been working as a professor with the RTA School of Media at Ryerson University in Toronto, Canada for eight years after several years as a television and radio journalist. I was teaching writing, documentary production and on-camera presentation skills.

As head of the student exchange program for my department at Ryerson University (Ryerson University changed its name to Toronto Metropolitan University in 2022 due to recognition of Egerton Ryerson's participation in the Canadian indigenous residential school system), I saw how students benefited from going on exchanges. The international experience opened their minds and affected everything from their world view to personal development, increased confidence and motivation and expanded their ideas about their future careers. I realized that only a few students got that international experience. It's expensive to go on exchange and a limited number of students are accepted by each exchange partner. I looked for a way to give as many students as possible the chance to interact with their peers in other countries.

I contacted universities where Ryerson already had student exchange programs and proposed the idea of working together to produce news and current affairs programs with students creating video stories and interviews on the same theme. The first iteration in 2000 was called *The Virtual Newsroom* and included universities in Germany, New Zealand and the UK. The students produced video stories about environmental change in their countries.

Back then, the biggest problem was that technology had not caught up to the idea. It's difficult to collaborate if you can't easily and quickly communicate with each other. It was impossible at that time to send large video files online, so all of the participants had to ship VHS tapes in the mail. Email was the only method of communication, and that involved delays because of the time zone differences.

After that first attempt, the project took a hiatus of several years. I spent time researching universities around the world that had media production and journalism programs with a strong emphasis on practice-based learning. I travelled to several countries, met with faculty members and worked through how we would each include a collaborative production in our existing curricula, deal with different time zones, evaluate the students' work and get the students to go beyond just producing videos in their own locations. The goal was to collaborate and work with one another to produce current affairs shows.

The project started up again in 2009 under the name The Global Campus Network. Our motto was, "Local voices, international perspectives." The objective was to tell stories that were universally interesting and important for university students and to examine the different ways those stories are viewed around the world.

Go to bit.ly/Ch4GCS1 to see the promotional video from *The Global Campus Network* (Global Journalism Collaboration, 2023a).

Participating universities

In 2009, Ryerson students worked with students at universities in the UK, Israel, Brazil, the U.S. and Hong Kong. Over the years, some partners dropped out as professors retired or changed jobs. Other partners were added including universities in the Netherlands, Taiwan and South Africa.

Some countries had excellent journalism and media production programs but could not participate because of restrictions in their curriculum. One country was not able to participate because of government censorship that would have made it impossible for their students to contribute.

As the project evolved, so did its name. After several iterations, it is now known as Global Campus Studio Productions (GCSP).

Themes

Each semester faculty from the participating universities come up with a theme. Over the years the shows have explored topics such as beauty and how it is defined differently around the world, student adaptation during the early days of COVID, food waste, fake news and transportation.

In the beauty show, the co-hosts participated in an interesting discussion on piercing and tattooing, and how it is perceived around the world.

In the transportation show, students in each country drove a car, rode a bike or took public transit from home to their universities and then discussed traffic congestion, the public transit systems in each city and how some cities are not bike friendly.

In the food show, the students co-hosts sampled foods from other countries that they had never eaten including Canadian poutine (french fries covered in gravy and cheese curds) and Australian Vegemite.

Go to bit.ly/Ch4GCS2 to watch a story from the *Food for Thought* show about the diversity of foods in Israel (Global Journalism Collaboration, 2023b).

In the fake news show, students looked at stories that had gone viral on social media and discussed whether they were real or fake news.

In 2020, GCSP produced a series of shows called *Let's Talk Racism*. It was at the time that police officers killed George Floyd in the United States and protests erupted around the world as a result. One of the students at Breda University in the Netherlands reported on a 19th-century Christmas tradition called Black Pete that faced a lot of criticism in the last few decades. The hosts from the other countries had not heard of this tradition and had a serious and open-minded discussion about how traditions such as Black Pete need to be re-examined. Go to bit.ly/Ch4GCS6 to see the website for *Let's Talk Racism* (Let's Talk Racism website, n.d.).

The *Let's Talk Racism* show also examined the Bihari people in India who face ongoing discrimination and the students in Hong Kong discussed the discrimination mainland migrants to Hong Kong face when looking for a job.

Go to bit.ly/Ch4GCS3 to watch a story from the *Let's Talk Racism* show produced by students in India about the Bihari people (Global Campus Studio Productions, 2021).

The process

How GCSP works

Before the semester starts, Zoom or other video conferencing platforms are used to meet with the instructors from the partner universities. A date for the show is set, we discuss and agree on a theme, and we come up with a list of possible topics that would relate to that theme.

Students work within the guidelines of their own universities. Instructors communicate the selected theme to the students. The students then work with their own professors to develop stories. They use the topic list as a guideline and often come up with their own, original ideas.

Faculty and students encounter several obstacles when working with international partners including using different words for the same technical term. In Canada, a recorded three-minute video is called a story. Other locations call the same thing videos, films, VTs or packages. So, one of the first steps in international collaboration is to agree on the terminology or at least provide a chart showing the different terms used in different countries and their meanings.

Format

The stories are three minutes maximum and follow a typical news format with the reporter's voice overs and short interview clips. As well, students conduct separate five-minute interviews with local experts based on the chosen theme.

Students can record their interviews and their voice overs in their own language and then include subtitles. GCSP has produced stories in Cantonese, Dutch, Danish, Hebrew, Mandarin, Portuguese, Russian and other languages with corresponding subtitles in English.

Go to bit.ly/Ch4GCS4 to watch a story produced by students from Metodista University in Brazil about homelessness. The story is in Portuguese with English subtitles (Global Journalism Collaboration, 2023c).

In 2022, Katherine Blair from Leeds Trinity University in the UK took the helm and produced a GCSP show called *And The Good News Is*. She required subtitles on all video stories, including those already produced in English as well as adding them to the overall program. Katherine thought it was only fair that everyone else included subtitles because of a growing sense of making our programs as accessible as possible, but also because young people in particular tend to watch TV with subtitles even when watching in their native language (YouGov, UK, 2023).

Some students are tasked with doing background research on the chosen theme to provide additional information for the hosts to discuss during the show. The research could include statistics, graphs, maps or photographs that add depth to the discussions.

Taking the lead

It's important for one university to take on the role of executive producer and be in charge of coordinating communications and meetings, preparing a Google Drive folder (or other means of sharing data) with all the relevant documents, and making sure all of the videos and scripts are submitted. The lead university is also in charge of the technical side of the show, communicating with the partners about all aspects of creating a show in a television studio. Since 2009, I've had the lead role of executive producer from Toronto.

Throughout the production process, the students are in communication with one another. Students at the lead university write the show scripts. To do that, they have to communicate with their peers to find out what they are working on and how those stories will fit into the shows. Each student writes an introduction to his/her story indicates the length of the story and whether it is in English or has subtitles. Once the script is ready, it is shared with the partners, who then have an opportunity to suggest changes. Here is an example of the opening few pages from one of the *Food for Thought* shows (Table 4.1).

Table 4.1 Food for thought script

1	SOT: SHOW OPENING	0:20	
2	Shae Hayes Ryerson Univ Canada Noa Yakabov TAU,Israel Nativ Kadmon Kozlov TAU, Israel Yvonne Chung and Gigi Chong, HKBU, Hong Kong Abbie Lord Leeds Trinity Univ		Shae/Ryerson: Hello and welcome to Food for Thought a series of shows produced by university students from around the world. I'm Shae Hayes, from Ryerson University, Toronto. Noa/Israel: I'm Noa Yakobov along with Nativ Kadmon Kozlov Nativ/Israel: We're from TAU in Israel. Gigi/HKBU: I am Gigi Chong with Yvonne Chung at Hong Kong Baptist University in Hong Kong. Yvonne/HKBU: This is one of seven shows that we've produced all of which can be found on our website and social media. Abbie/Leeds: And, I'm Abbie Lords from Leeds university in the UK. Our show today will talk about sustainable eating with a focus on meat and dairy alternatives.
3			Gigi/HK: Our first story takes place here in Hong Kong. Processed vegetarian products are becoming increasingly popular here nowadays. Yvonne/HKBU: There are new shops and restaurants that sell and serve a variety of these plant based meals. But are they as good as the manufacturers claim? Phoebe Law reports.
4	SOT HKBU Law Omnipork	1:20	SOT HKBU Law Omnipork runs 2:52
5	B roll photo of GreenCommon Market in Hong Kong b roll photo of A and W Beyond meat burger	4:12	Gigi/HK: Omnipork seems to be a good meat substitute with high protein content for vegetarians or people who are giving up meat. I've tasted Omnipork once before but it's not widely available in Hong Kong's wet market, only at particular vegetarian shops offering plant-based meat. Yvonne/HKBU: Shae, how about in Canada? Is plant-based meat popular there? Shae/Ryerson: Plant based meat is popular and you can find it in grocery stories...I like something called 'beyond meat' at one of our fast food restaurants A and W.

(*Continued*)

Table 4.1 (Continued)

	Abbie/Leeds: (say whether you have tried anything like omnipork and what you think about plant based foods that taste like meat) Then say: Noa and Nativ, how about you? **Noa or Nativ/Israel:** (give your opinion on plant based foods that taste like meat) **Noa/Israel:** Moving on, Israel is considered the most vegan country in the world. Over 5% of Israelis claim to be vegan. In fact, Israel has recently pocketed its new nickname "vegan nation". **Nativ/Israel:** On top of that, Israel's reputation for its impressive start-up culture cannot go unnoticed. In proportion to its population, Israel has the largest number of startup companies in the world. **Noa/Israel:** Our reporters found one particular start-up that merges these two worlds. Focusing on their passion for veganism and sustainability, they created "remilk"; a new and unique technological approach to non-dairy products. Over to Shai Bauminger at Tel Aviv University with the story.

Sometimes we have so many video stories to choose from, we produce more than one show on the same topic. We've had many discussions about whether young people are willing to watch a 90-minute show on YouTube or Facebook. As a result, we've created subtopics within our show theme and produced shorter shows that range from 15 minutes to 45 minutes. In the *Let's Talk Racism* series, there were six shows ranging from discussions about activism and education to stories about personal experiences with racism. In the *Food For Thought* series, students produced separate shows on food waste, nutrition, agriculture and a celebration of foods from around the world.

After the stories are produced and the scripts are written, it's time to produce the shows. We create a call sheet or chart, so everyone knows when to show up.

Since 2020, we've had a website, Global-Campus, (global-campus.org), where visitors can watch entire shows or watch individual stories. As well, we post the shows on Facebook and YouTube.

Hosts

Each university selects students to co-host the shows. Co-hosting television shows is challenging even for experienced presenters who are working side by side in the same studio. Many students have little or no experience being on camera and have to quickly develop a camaraderie with co-hosts in other countries, who they can only see on a TV monitor.

I provide a presentation skills workshop where we rehearse the scripts and go over tips and hints for giving a natural and conversational on-camera performance.

One of the collaborative aspects of the GCSP shows is the interaction between the hosts. The goal is not to simply have each host read an introduction to a story produced by a peer at their university but to have something to say to one another once that story has aired.

The shows are hosted in English, which can be a challenge as students in some countries are not fluent. Some students do well reading the script but struggle to ad lib during the more conversational parts of the shows. Many of the professors have years of experience in TV news and current affairs. They also provide rehearsals so their student hosts can be well prepared.

Technology

From 2009 until the start of COVID-19 in 2020, most of our shows were produced live and streamed on YouTube and Facebook. We used technology called Haivision (Chapter 10) and Professional Skype. Some shows were pre-recorded because they had complex graphics and additional information that needed to be added in post-production.

Most of the shows ran smoothly but in the early days of Skype, we faced a few technical problems. Sometimes connections would be lost or we could hear students at a particular location but not see them and vice versa.

Once the pandemic shut down universities worldwide, we switched to Zoom. Because it was difficult to incorporate all of the production elements into a Zoom show (such as graphics, photographs and subtitles), we recorded the host segments and edited everything else in post-production. That meant adding photographs, maps, statistics, graphics and music.

Collaborating

The student co-hosts benefit most from getting to know and talk to one another. We continue to work on ways for all of the students to collaborate with their peers. In an effort to do that, Katherine Blair from Leeds Trinity University and Faith Sidlow from California State University, Fresno, initiated an idea to share story pitches. In one case, students from Canada met on Zoom and pitched their ideas to students in California, and vice versa. Then, they critiqued each other's pitches. In another case, students produced one-minute videos pitching their ideas and then watched pitches from another country and recorded their own video feedback.

Another collaborative technique is the co-interview. Students in Toronto found someone to interview in Canada and then partnered with a student from another country who got involved as a second interviewer, bringing an international perspective to the topic being discussed.

One year, we produced a live eSports tournament that ended with students from London Southbank University in the UK engaging in a discussion with students from Ryerson University in Toronto about the growing popularity of eSports around the world.

Challenges

As noted, in the early days, technology was a problem because it was difficult to send large files, and Skype did not always work consistently.

In all international collaborations, time zone differences are a big issue. If you are including partners in Australia, North America, South America, Europe and Asia, some students will have to start very early and others will have to stay up very late. That can make it difficult to access TV studios if the university is closed at certain times.

As well as time zone differences, universities have different semester and holiday schedules. We've found that late October/early November and late April/early May are the only times of the year when almost everyone around the world is on campus. We moved the show date for GCSP to November a few years ago, and that made it harder for Brazil, Australia and South Africa to take part because their semester is almost over by then. One solution is to create a 12-month production schedule, come up with the next theme in January and allow partners to create their stories throughout the year and save them until the shows are produced.

In a professional newsroom, stories are assigned and reporters have to produce those exact stories. That's not always the case in university projects. Some students change their story ideas and don't communicate that to the host university which necessitates making last-minute changes to the script. Some students produce stories that are too long to fit into the show and have to be shortened. Others don't send in their stories on time.

It's important that only a few people have control over making changes in scripts and call sheets. Once, someone made a change and didn't inform the other partners, and as a result, students from one country showed up two hours early to record the show.

Another year, students from one location made script changes without informing the other partners and that delayed the show because we weren't all using the same script. We found that adjusting the settings in the shared documents so only specific people could edit helped control who was making changes to the scripts.

All the GCSP instructors have agreed that undergraduate participants want to be sure that their work is graded, otherwise, they consider it extra work and are often not motivated to complete it. At Toronto Metropolitan University, we assess the students on all aspects of the production process so they are keen to complete the work.

It's also challenging when faculty members retire or leave their universities. Projects like GCSP require instructors who are passionate about taking part and willing to spend the time required to communicate with partner universities around the world. It often takes new instructors a while to understand how international collaborations work and how they will incorporate such projects into their existing curriculum. The projects also challenge instructors to think creatively about how they incorporate such projects into their existing curriculum. The extra effort that's required doesn't appeal to everyone.

Benefits

Working on GCSP shows gives students the opportunity to see how people in other countries live and how they think about and react to current issues.

Students also rise to the occasion because they are trying to show their best selves to their international counterparts. They see the project as a tangible creation rather than just a classroom exercise. They also benefit from interacting with students beyond national borders giving them a sense that the world is not as vast as it may seem when they are all collaborating on the same project.

When students produce work for an international audience, they have to think about how to explain something that is typically Canadian or South African or Israeli to an audience who may not understand their local culture.

Students rarely get to see work done by students in other countries. The experience of working on GCSP shows allows them to look at the differences and similarities in how we produce video stories around the world. Every year, our regular group of partners has been enthusiastic about taking part again.

References

Global Campus Studio Productions. (2021). *MITSFT history of Biharis India 1*. [Video]. YouTube. Retrieved from https://www.youtube.com/watch?v=C0BD5dYXfk8&ab_channel=GlobalCampusStudioProductions

Global Journalism Collaboration. (2023a). *Ch4GCS1- Global campus network promotional video*. [Video]. YouTube. Retrieved from https://www.youtube.com/watch?v=YiYdSHRqDdM&list=PLU8114WOh4VLKFqgwbHY2sgBJtkDgour9

Global Journalism Collaboration. (2023b). *CH4GCS2- Food for thought - Diversity of food in Israel*. [Video]. YouTube. Retrieved from https://www.youtube.com/watch?v=y CAm-vms PEQ&ab_channel=GlobalJournalismCollaboration

Global Journalism Collaboration. (2023c). *Ch4GCS4- Food for Thought - Homelessness in Brazil*. [Video]. YouTube. Retrieved from https://www.youtube.com/watch? v=uVVT-PLONv0&list=PLU8114WOh4VLKFqgwbHY2sgBJtkDgour9&index=3L et's Talk Racism: Global Campus Studio Productions. (n.d.). [website]. Retrieved from https://branched-count-6aa.notion.site/478129122d9540f0b1b218fb4ee14f67?v=c7adc96e978842a9932bbb11c6709c13

YouGov UK. (2023, February 24). When watching TV shows or movies in your native language, do you generally prefer to have the subtitles on or off? *yougov.co.uk*. Retrieved from https://yougov.co.uk/topics/media/survey-results/daily/2023/02/24/9a34f/3

5 The Global Pop-Up Newsroom

David Baines and Devadas Rajaram

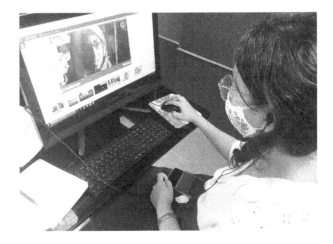

Figure 5.1 Global Pop-Up Newsroom, Asian College of Journalism, Chennai, India.

Concept

Since 2013, the Global Pop-Up Newsroom has brought together student and working journalists around the world twice a year to report on critical social concerns using only social media platforms and mobile technologies such as phones, tablets and laptops.

In the November/December iteration, the theme is a chosen topic and in March, reports focus on International Women's Day and culminate on March 8. The intention was to create an experimental, ephemeral, virtual space in which participants facilitate, promote and curate conversations which explore complexity, synthesise the local and the global and bring to the fore the voices of those who often go unheard.

The purpose of the Global Pop-Up Newsroom was to invite and encourage students preparing for careers in journalism, a field constantly disrupted, to challenge long-standing boundaries. These boundaries characterised

DOI: 10.4324/9781003428725-6

journalism practice and education, reinforcing divisions between amateur and professional, producer and consumer and product and process. These divisions were epitomised by the "newsroom," which created barriers between journalists, news consumers and the communities they aim to serve and represent.

The newsroom has long been recognised as a place where journalism's entrants are socialised into the values, cultures and ideologies of a profession informed by particular models of media ownership and hierarchical social structures (Gans, 1979; Domingo, 2008) that fostered group-centric, self-referential perspectives on society and the role of journalism and journalists in those societies (Tuchman, 1978; Deuze, 2008; Wall, 2015).

And yet, while the field was undergoing such extensive disruption and dislocation, the globally dominant model of journalism education remained one which sought to reproduce the newsroom as the paradigm for professional practice. But things were changing. Some journalism educators were calling for a paradigm shift for the adoption of community-centric, experimental approaches that encouraged students to question, innovate and explore new ways to do journalism and rethink relationships between journalist and audience (Mensing, 2010; Berger, 2011; Robinson, 2013; Baines and Li, 2013).

Participating universities

It was at this moment of inflection in journalism education in 2013 that the Global Pop-Up Newsroom was born out of a happy coincidence at the Third World Journalism Education Congress (WJEC) in Mechelen, Belgium. Melissa Wall, of California State University, Northridge (CSUN), was presenting on the Pop-Up Newsroom project she ran with her students in Los Angeles, California, U.S., and David Baines was in the same session, presenting on the *Jesmond Local* hyperlocal journalism project, which he and colleague Ian Wylie initiated at Newcastle University in the UK. Both were "laboratories of inquiry" (Mensing, 2010, p. 512) in which journalism students abandoned the traditional newsroom to reposition themselves in their communities.

A dislocation later captured in the phrase "we are where you are" (Baines et al., 2016) to mark the manner in which digitised news erodes distinctions between producers and consumers of information in the creation of networked journalism (Bruns, 2008; Heinrich, 2011; Russell, 2011).

Wall and Baines immediately saw the attraction of taking the Pop-Up project global. Wall had sent her students into the community to report using cell phones and Twitter on events as diverse as Los Angeles' annual no-car day, CicLAvia and The Oscars and to tell the compelling stories of those who used the long-distance buses in America.

Events were difficult to map into academic timetables, so the first iteration in November 2013 was a focus on poverty, austerity and deprivation with 127 student participants from CSUN, Newcastle and the Asian College of Journalism in Chennai, India, with a team led by Devadas Rajaram and another from National Chung Cheng University, Taiwan.

Since then, it has also drawn participants in various years from Dhaka University, Bangladesh; Mariupol University, Ukraine; California State University, Fresno, U.S.; Marquette University, Milwaukee, U.S.; University of Oregon, U.S; Rafik Hariri University, Lebanon; the University of Applied Sciences, Utrecht; the University of Groningen, Holland; Stuttgart Media University, Germany; University of Vienna, Austria; University of Padova, Italy; Complutense University of Madrid, Spain; Universidade de São Paulo, Brazil; the American University in Bulgaria; the American University in Cairo, Egypt and Coventry University, UK. It has also involved independent journalists working in Nepal, Bhutan, Pakistan, Sri Lanka, Afghanistan, Armenia, Kenya, Zimbabwe, Ghana, Romania, Germany and Brazil.

Themes

The project embraces two critical and related themes: social justice and giving a voice to those who go unheard. To that end, the iterations in November/ December each year have focused, among other topics, on poverty, food, the drive to eliminate violence against women and girls, the climate crisis, the defence of human rights, migration and refugees. And in March each year, the focus is on International Women's Day and the myriad concerns that emerge in the global conversations that burst forth on and around March 8.

It has featured homeless people on the streets of Los Angeles, destitute widows in India, and people who have been forced from their homes by conflict and by the climate crisis.

But the project has also been increasingly informed by the tenets of solutions journalism. Its purpose is not simply to highlight social injustices but to provide information from a wide range of local and global perspectives and to challenge those injustices and facilitate connections that help people build a more equitable world. So it has also brought people of power and influence, politicians and policy makers, into the conversations.

Process

How the Pop-Up Newsroom works

Mark Deuze, citing Sigmund Bauman, pictures our social world as "a liquid modern society […] one where uncertainty, flux, change, conflict, and revolution are the permanent conditions of everyday life" (2008, p. 22). Journalism, in consequence, is a field in a similarly "liquid" state.

The Global Pop-Up Newsroom, as a space of inquiry and experimentation in journalism, has undergone multiple transformations. In its first iteration, students shared a central Twitter account (@PopUpNewsroom) and decided on a shared hashtag (#LivePoverty). They reported live from the field using their mobile phones, and the cascade of posts from around the world were curated on a free RebelMouse account.

Analysis by TweetReach at the time revealed that over 48 hours, #LivePoverty gained 386,541 impressions—the tweets were delivered to that many Twitter accounts—and the account was being followed by the UN in India and by UNESCO, among others.

The operation on that day had taken a considerable degree of forward planning and collaboration between the participating student teams. The U.S. team at CSUN, on Pacific Standard Time, kicked off on the afternoon of November 15, then passed control of the Twitter account to the ACJ in Chennai, who later passed control to Newcastle, who eventually passed it back to CSUN early on their Saturday morning.

Throughout the operation, students from each school monitored, followed and reposted content from the others. In the years since, roughly the same format has been maintained, but some universities have preferred to prepare content in advance and schedule it to post on the day of the event on YouTube and Twitter.

Others have prepared some content in advance and delivered some live on the day. Others have set up websites to host, curate and archive content. RebelMouse was dropped after a few years as a curation platform because it moved to a paid service with high fees.

And more recently, the central focus has shifted from X, formerly known as Twitter, to a Facebook Live stream coordinated by the ACJ team in Chennai using the streaming platform BeLive.

It is fair to say that the recent innovations in delivery of the Global Pop-Up Newsroom and the scoping and testing of new platforms and media technologies has been led by the dynamic team in India. But the original format is still recognisable as the project passes from anchors in one school to anchors in another, and each segment features live and prepared content from each school's region. It still engages locally and globally with issues of social justice and it still focuses on giving a voice to those who go unheard.

The most recent International Women's Day iteration at the time of writing featured segments hosted by women journalists in Afghanistan who were suffering persecution and often physical attacks at the hands of the ruling Taliban government and by journalism staff and students from Mariupol University in Ukraine, whose campus and city had been destroyed by invading Russian forces. A recording of the five-hour livestream is available at this link: bit.ly/Ch5IWD23

Challenges

New platforms and technologies have increasingly challenged geographical boundaries for journalism, and critical social concerns such as the climate crisis, pandemics, poverty, conflict and migration are manifested both locally and globally.

Journalism, traditionally a competitive enterprise, is becoming increasingly collaborative with journalists more often coordinating with colleagues internationally. In early iterations of the project, students could take part very much as an individual enterprise delivering their own content and posting links to it on the shared account with the agreed hashtag.

But it was intended from the beginning to be a trans-global collaboration. Students participating in more recent iterations of the Global Pop-Up Newsroom have found they have to work collaboratively with colleagues in their groups locally and globally to deliver the project on the day of the programme.

The processes and practices of collaboration are important in terms of the learning which this project delivers, as the content produced and the global conversations that are generated. Bringing together students from different universities and different parts of the world helps to create a journalism that is both more nuanced and impactful.

Another challenge has been the need to accommodate the project within diverse learning and teaching traditions in different countries and different institutional structures and academic calendars. From a pedagogical perspective, learning to collaborate with others is a valuable outcome of this exercise.

It has proved virtually impossible to extend participation to countries in the southern hemisphere because academic years follow different cycles. In the north, the year begins in September, in the south, in late January or February.

When students in some institutions are in the midst of a teaching period, others are in an assessment period and are too focused on exams or completing assignments to take part in an extracurricular activity.

Some institutions have the flexibility within their procedures to accommodate the project as an additional assignment for which the students will earn credits towards their qualification. In others, assignments and assessments are published long in advance and there is not that flexibility.

So some schools can embrace the project as a compulsory activity for their students; in others it has to remain an extra-curricular activity in which participation is voluntary. This puts hurdles in the way of those collaborations in which students in different institutions might work together to produce a particular piece of media content. If one is doing it voluntarily, the stakes for her may not be as high as for another who is working towards a grade that will have significance for their successful completion of their course of study.

National holidays vary from country to country, and this has from time to time caused difficulties in scheduling the November/December iteration because the important Thanksgiving holiday falls on the fourth Thursday in November in the U.S. Following that, there are often only two teaching weeks left before universities in the UK break up for Christmas in mid-December—weeks that often include assignment submission dates.

On one occasion, the students wanted to run the November/December iteration on the annual Day to Eliminate Violence Against Women and Girls. Unfortunately, the United Nations had chosen November 25 for this day, so journalism schools in the U.S. were prevented from participating because it clashed with the Thanksgiving holiday.

Benefits

Students who participate learn to work across cultures and to collaborate with their classmates and with others in different parts of the world. They become immersed in the communities they are reporting on and for and soon find themselves seeking a diversity of voices. They learn to approach journalism as a laboratory of inquiry in which to advance their knowledge, develop their skills and practices and explore opportunities to innovate and work creatively. These are all important lessons to learn when preparing for a career in a constantly changing, shifting, liquid world of media work.

It benefits the journalism schools which participate as opportunities emerge to develop relationships and engagements with schools in other parts of the world. And it benefits faculty members in those schools who draw on these relationships to learn from each other and to expand, diversify and internationalise their curricula and the delivery of their programmes.

What's next?

One of the key characteristics of the Global Pop-Up Newsroom has been its flexibility and ability to shape-shift and adapt and maintain its relevance in journalism education and to adapt to the changing worlds of journalism, changing needs of the participating J-schools and their students, and to maintain a focus on the critical global concerns with which our societies are struggling.

Participants have joined and left, and others have come along and brought with them new insights, fresh perspectives and innovative approaches. And the centre of gravity has shifted. While it has maintained its global reach—accepting its rootedness in the northern hemisphere for reasons outlined above—in the most recent iterations a clear majority of the voices it has brought to the fire have been from the Indian sub-continent and neighbouring countries and from African nations. It has become a showcase for exciting, vigorous, creative and engaged journalism that is thriving there.

So, what's next is more of the same—the Global Pop-Up Newsroom will continue to evolve, continue to be relevant and continue to excite journalism students and their teachers.

References

Baines, D., & Li, T. (2013, June). *Students teaching in the community: Building employability, social sustainability and "journalism as process."* Paper presented at the World Journalism Education Conference, Mechelen, Belgium.

Baines, D., Rajasekar, P., van Kerkhoven, M., & Wall, M. (2016). Pop-Up newsroom: "We are where you are." *Medium*: [Civic media project.] Retrieved from https://

medium.com/civic-media-project/ pop-up-newsroom-we-are-where-you-are-8870c c58603f

Berger, G. (2011). Empowering the youth as citizen journalists: A South African experience. *Journalism*, *12*(6), 708–726. doi:10.1177/1464884911405466

Bruns, A. (2008). *Blogs, Wikipedia, second life, and beyond: From production to produsage.* New York: Peter Lang.

Deuze, M. (2008). The changing context of news work: Liquid journalism for a monitorial citizenry. *International Journal of Communication*, *2*, 18.

Domingo, D. (2008). Interactivity in the daily routines of online newsrooms: Dealing with an uncomfortable myth. *Journal of Computer-Mediated Communication*, *13*(3), 680–704.

Gans, H. J. (1979). *Deciding what's news: A study of CBS Evening News, NBC Nightly News, Newsweek, and Time.* Evanston, IL: Northwestern University Press.

Heinrich, A. (2011). *Network journalism: Journalistic practice in interactive spheres.* New York: Routledge.

Mensing, D. (2010). Rethinking [again] the future of journalism education. *Journalism Studies*, *11*(4), 511–523.

Robinson, S. (2013). Teaching "journalism as process": A proposed paradigm for J-school curricula in the digital age. *Teaching Journalism & Mass Communication*, *3*(1), 1–12.

Russell, A. (2011). *Networked: A contemporary history of news in transition.* Malden, MA: Polity.

Tuchman, G. (1978). *Making news; A study of the construction of reality.* New York: Free Press.

Wall, M. (2015). Change the space, change the practice? Re-imagining journalism education with the Pop-Up Newsroom. *Journalism Practice*, *9*(2), 123–137.

6 Global E-News Immersion Initiative (GENII)

Priya Rajasekar

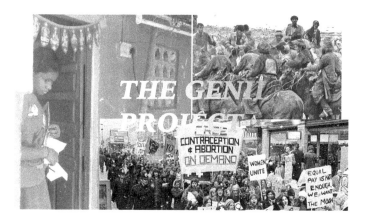

Figure 6.1 Global E-News Immersion Initiative, Coventry University, UK.

It was late afternoon in Coventry, UK, and journalism students on the GENII project (Global E-News Immersion Initiative) were due to meet their counterpart from Fresno State University via Zoom. At 4:30 a.m. PST, Monica (name changed) was already busy working in a barn caring for her horses. My students and I watched transfixed as Monica expertly tended to her horses and cleaned the barn. Bucket in one hand and phone in the other, she breathlessly shared details of her daily routine as she showed us around in the dark just before sunrise in her part of the world in Fresno, California.

Monica was due to work as remote reporter and editor on a story set in Coventry while her GENII project partner was to work with her on a story set in Fresno. Neither had physically travelled to these places before.

Earlier in 2016, we were hosting the first iteration of GENII. The theme was ageing and related lifestyles. A student from Coventry had just recorded his interview with an elderly woman who stayed at a refugee camp in Lebanon. Support from his project partner, a student at Rafik Hariri University, had been invaluable in setting up this interview. The student said he was moved to

DOI: 10.4324/9781003428725-7

tears as he narrated how the lady in question had matter-of-factly said that she and her partner willingly starved so their grandchildren in the refugee camp could eat better. Their lives are more important, she had said. The student knew what that really meant. He had arrived on the shores of the UK some years ago as an asylum seeker.

Moments like these are important in our work as educators to recognise the often-intangible value of the work that we do and the difference it makes in the lives of our students.

The concept

GENII is inspired by the Pop-Up Newsroom project (Chapter 5), which has been live for over a decade and involves students from around the world producing stories using their mobile phones to "pop up" newsrooms anywhere and at any time, breaking free from the dependence on traditional spaces designated as news rooms (Wall, 2015). Participating in one of the earliest iterations of the project as an educator at the Asian College of Journalism in Chennai, India, I witnessed how it opened a new world of collaborative online journalism projects at the institution and also served as a springboard for similar initiatives, including the Global News Relay (Chapters 3 and 4) and ACJ Engage, a project executed in collaboration with UNICEF, where citizens from around the country were invited to contribute stories on children's issues by sharing multimedia content through a mobile app developed for the purpose.

Later, as an academic at Coventry University, I learnt that a large percentage of my students had never left England (including one student who had never been on a train). The university, through the Erasmus programme (pre-Brexit) and through paid student international trips, aimed to address this to an impressive extent, but the challenge was to find a way to harness technology to ensure that such international experience was more accessible and more widely available while also being embedded in the curriculum.

In addition to the opportunity to travel (virtually) to a geographically distanced location, GENII would, I hoped, allow students to explore independently while giving them access to spaces and regions, including those not often considered safe for international travel, even as they practised their journalism as they would in their place of study. GENII also went beyond directed student trips. International student trips largely involve planned visits and tours with limited resources, scope and time for independent journalistic exploration and is further subject to risk assessment and management.

The motivation for GENII was driven by an academic intent to decolonise the curriculum. The call for an ontological approach to journalism has been strengthening over the years (Mutsvairo, Borges-Rey et al., 2021; Deuze & Witschge, 2018). While broad ethics and journalistic principles are generally accepted and valued, the practice and profession of journalism is not immune to epistemic and ontological influences, an aspect that continues to be under-researched, under-explored in classrooms and underfunded through research and teaching grants (Glück, 2018).

The domination of Eurocentric ideas and thinking in journalism education and practice, coupled with the impact of Global North-South geopolitics, is evident both in academia and in newsrooms. This limits the opportunity for students to gain a more holistic understanding of diverse socio-economic and political perspectives and nuanced approaches to journalism scholarship and practice.

GENII endeavours to energise and inspire students to critically engage with some of these questions through fieldwork and experimentation that exposes them to the diversity and complexity of journalistic practice in different parts of the world.

The concept of GENII is based on a reimagination of geographical location by harnessing digital and social media technology. GENII enables student reporters to cover stories in a geographically distanced location through peer-to-peer collaboration and reciprocal field support.

While the student lead retains editorial rights and is able to determine the angle, flow, format, medium and structure of the story, their peer at the location where the story is set offers support as their eyes and ears, helping with identifying sources on the ground, travelling to the location of the source or story as directed, recording audio and video interviews conducted by the lead reporter via digital tools, offering interpretation where relevant, etc.

GENII builds on the potential and ambition of online collaborative projects by going beyond compilation of stories produced by journalism students from around the world on a shared online space to facilitating geographically distanced fieldwork and reporting through the use of digital and social media technology.

The idea behind GENII is to offer students the opportunity to immerse and report on the ground as though they are physically there. Opportunities include talking to potential sources in a geographically distanced location, learning about a new culture first hand, working on a common theme as part of an international student community and gaining an understanding of common global challenges through an exposure to plural, multicultural perspectives and experiences. Key transferable skills such as the use of digital and social media technology, opportunity to improvise and creatively use available technological tools under less-than-ideal conditions, problem-solving, communication skills, teamwork and reflection are also part of the student learning journey.

The rationale for the project, which I conceptualised during my tenure as journalism educator, was to expand student understanding of critical socio-economic and political issues and provide them with opportunities to collaborate and report virtually from geographically distanced locations. Applying journalistic principles and ethics, exploring diverse and decolonised approaches to journalism and reporting on key global issues and challenges were core drivers for the project.

In hindsight, working in the area of sustainability, the replicability and scalability of GENII to other academic disciplines is increasingly evident to me. Through such remote immersed learning and co-creation, which has also become more accessible, normal and refined in the wake of the COVID-19 pandemic, the inter- and trans-disciplinary potential of projects such as GENII to enhance student learning and encourage hands-on participation in tackling global challenges such as climate change and associated social and environmental injustice is worthy of further exploration. From a learning design perspective, GENII also facilitates applied learning, action research and the use of technology to provide transformative student experiences.

The process

Planning and executing GENII

The translation of GENII from concept to execution and outcome relied on the enthusiasm and efforts of colleagues in participating institutions. Virtual planning and brainstorming sessions across time zones was inevitably outside normal working hours for many colleagues. Some of the early tasks included the identification of themes, gauging the number of student participants at each institution, determining the size of each team, ensuring a fair representation of students across all participating institutions and regions to ensure an optimisation of cross-cultural learning, accommodating students with learning disabilities, considering aspects of ethics (consent, safety, privacy, use of social media), etc.

For the pilot iteration of GENII involving students from Germany, Lebanon, the U.S., and the UK, we chose the theme of ageing and related lifestyles and challenges. From speaking to interviewees in care homes in England and Germany to learning about the life of the elderly in Lebanon's refugee camps, students were given the opportunity to understand and explore the theme from diverse angles and learn from their collective experiences and stories.

Other practical considerations included the mapping of the project to the curriculum and associated assessment tasks by each participating institution. Allocating time to plan and schedule the project was also given due consideration. Participating academics had the opportunity to design assignment tasks in line with their course curriculum.

While the pilot was not assessed, in subsequent iterations as a way to encourage more active contribution, students were assessed on participation and the submission of a reflection essay by a majority of participating institutions. As the successful completion of the project depended on variables such as cooperation from peers, timely response of potential sources, technological challenges etc., it was decided by a majority of the participating institutions that the content itself would not be graded.

In addition, other tasks included the storage of multimedia content produced by students on a shared Google Drive and a dedicated Facebook group (for each iteration) managed by participating academics who also posted scholarly resources for students and collated consent forms for multimedia recording. Initial group introductions involved shared virtual sessions where students also had the opportunity to interact with and learn from participating tutors. One iteration also benefited from a workshop hosted by Google News Lab.

Students were then encouraged to get in touch with their designated project team using social media tools such as WhatsApp and Facebook. A Facebook closed group created for each iteration of the project allowed students to ask questions, share resources and initiate conversation on the project theme. Tutors used the space to offer guidance and encourage students to meet deadlines. Final stories were also posted to the community page, with a compilation put together on Medium (2019).

Since its pilot edition in 2016, GENII has gone through four successful iterations involving six universities and over 300 students (Albeanu, 2016). Project themes included lifestyle and culture (stories on food, culture, poverty, gender issues, caste, migration, sports, entertainment and so on), climate change and shelter. As a way to encourage students and acknowledge their efforts, printed certificates with the logos of participating universities were also distributed.

Benefits

The GENII experience

As academics collaborating on the project, our experience working on the Pop-Up Newsroom and Global News Relay had already helped us build a team that supported experimentation and co-creation. Any work of this nature depends on collective energies and commitment of tutors, and this project was no exception, the conception and design of which was in itself inspired by past experience working with and learning from colleagues.

As for students on the project, a Qualtrics survey in 2019 indicated that 90% of students felt the project enhanced their cross-cultural understanding. About 70% said they would like to participate again and a similar number said they would encourage a friend or junior classmember to participate.

Qualitative feedback and reflection were useful to understand the complexities and opportunities from a student perspective. While the idea appealed to most students, the difficulty working across time zones, understanding what was expected of them, juggling conflicting priorities and gaining collaborative support were some of the challenges highlighted.

A selection of positive phrases gleaned from student reflection and feedback include "really interesting experience", "marvellous opportunity to create global links", "opportunity to think out of the box and increased not only my employability, making me a global thinker but also changed my perception of the world", "enhanced my investigative and team skills", "idea and concept behind it fascinating and fun', 'important to know about local and global news', 'makes you more informed citizens", "I now realise that we have an entire planet of places to go to and see", "I can see that there are diverse ways of telling the same story" and "I think that student journalists from across the world have different techniques and story ideas" (Rajasekar, 2019).

Some of the phrases that highlighted the challenges students faced included "a bit confusing at first and took a while to lift off the ground", "Because I wasn't receiving a grade for the project, my motivation faded", "I would be getting messages at 3 am in the morning and too tired to reply."

Feedback from tutors working on the project (Rajasekar, 2019):

> The GENII project offered an exceptional opportunity to my students to work closely with other students from across the globe in what is likely to be an important model for international reporting in the future. The project is important both as a learning experience and a model for future journalists. It uses technology and collaborative, international teamwork to create an innovative approach to international reporting.
>
> The GENII project was a wonderful opportunity to engage with diverse communities and tell their stories through collaboration. It has been an exciting experience for my students to push the frontiers of storytelling. We should try to expand the project with more participants. In short, GENII was a huge learning curve for the students.

Challenges

GENII in the context of cross-border learning

Collaborative Online International Learning Projects (COIL) are immensely useful as a way to enhance the student learning journey. Such projects, if well planned and executed, go beyond ticking the box of internationalisation metrics that are now part of most league or ranking tables. They improve student access to diverse learning opportunities that expand cross-cultural understanding and experience, contribute to decolonising the curriculum and equip students with key transferable knowledge and skills. From a sustainability perspective, they are cost-effective, make optimum use of available digital and social media technology and are environmentally more sustainable (as opposed to air travel).

However, the crisis of neoliberalism that is impacting higher education (Fleming, 2021) also has a bearing on how these projects are conceived and executed and how they meet student expectations. There is also growing pressure on academics to deliver such projects and in juggling student expectation and project complexity, the quality of the project is at risk of compromise.

While it is unfair to both students and academics to be subject to such tensions, it is important to recognise the creativity, time and labour that both staff and students put in to ensure that a COIL project delivers real value. The overemphasis on grades and the expectation of students who often think of themselves as consumers (Calma & Dickson-Deane, 2020) entitled to high grades and an education that is considerate to pressures on their time (many working part time to afford fees and living expenses) is often a deterrent to innovation, improvisation and incompatible with the inevitable unpredictability and ad-hocness of such opportunities to work with students and academics in institutions around the world.

Working on GENII and similar projects has, on the one hand, been a way to work around some of these challenges and on the other, the very reason why such projects are so critical to the future of education. After all, without the pressure of an agenda-setting media chasing clicks and likes and the opportunity to experiment with like-minded academics and committed students, what better way can there be to tell cross-border stories that really matter?

References

Albeanu, C. (2016). The GENII project encourages student journalists from six countries to collaborate on stories. *Journalism.co.uk*. 28 November. [online] available from [6 June 2019].

Calma, A., & Dickson-Deane, C. (2020). The student as customer and quality in higher education. *International Journal of Educational Management. 34(8)*, 1221–1235

Deuze, M., & Witschge, T. (2018). Beyond journalism: Theorizing the transformation of journalism. *Journalism, 19*(2), 165–181.

Fleming, P. (2021). *Dark academia how universities die*. London: Pluto Press.

Glück, A. (2018). De-Westernization and decolonization in media studies. In *Oxford encyclopedia of communication and critical studies* (Oxford research encyclopedias). Oxford University Press. https://doi.org/10.1093/acrefore/9780190228613.013.898

Mutsvairo, B., Borges-Rey, E., Bebawi, S., Márquez-Ramírez, M., Mellado, C., Mabweazara, H. M., ... & Thussu, D. (2021). Ontologies of journalism in the Global South. *Journalism & Mass Communication Quarterly, 98*(4), 996–1016.

Rajasekar, P. (2019). The GENII project: Experimenting with a global collaborative journalism classroom. In C. Simmons (Ed.), *Teaching and learning excellence: The Coventry way: Case studies of tried and tested good practice in higher education*. Coventry, UK: Coventry University Group, 74–76. doi:10.18552/2019CUGCW1

Stories from the GENII project: Selection of stories published by students from six journalism schools around the world. (2019). *Medium*. Retrieved from https://medium.com/stories-from-the-genii-project

Wall, M. (2015). Change the space, change the practice? Re-imagining journalism education with the Pop-Up Newsroom. *Journalism Practice, 9*(2), 123–137.

7 Global Reporting Program (GRP)

Peter Klein and Britney Dennison

Figure 7.1 Global Reporting Program Student Monique Rodrigues Reporting on the Fishmeal Industry for *The Fish You (Don't Know You) Eat*, in Lima, Peru in 2018.

The Global Reporting Program (GRP) is a competitive entry, two-term graduate-level course at the University of British Columbia's School of Journalism, Writing, and Media. The programme is a hybrid classroom and field-work experience that brings together students, faculty, professional journalists and media organizations from around the world.

This model of collaborative learning and reporting across different countries fosters cross-cultural approaches to global journalism and provides students with real-world reporting experience and skills. Throughout the course, students study the norms and practices of global journalism with an emphasis towards critical analysis and innovation in the field of practice.

During the first term, students in the programme research, report and pitch stories; develop budgets and production schedules and lead field reporting. During the second term, students work collaboratively on post-production with their media partner through to publication.

DOI: 10.4324/9781003428725-8

The concept

Building a new approach

The GRP grew out of the International Reporting Program (IRP) at the University of British Columbia (UBC), a course launched in 2008 that trained more than 100 students in its first decade (UBC School of Journalism, n.d.). Past projects investigated illegal trade, government corruption and access to healthcare and medication, among other complex global issues. Reporting resulted in measurable impact, including arrests and policy changes.

Faculty and students spent time critiquing problematic "parachute reporting" practices with foreign reporters using local "fixers," who are often relegated to subservient, and sometimes even hidden, roles in international reporting (Plaut & Klein, 2021). At the same time, the nature of the programme – with ten Canadian-based graduate students travelling during their winter or spring break – necessitated some form of parachute reporting.

During the sixth year of IRP, the instructors decided to put theory into practice and truly challenge the parachute/fixer model, by experimenting with partnerships among students, removing the role of "fixers" and offering every participant equal opportunity for credit. In 2013–14, UBC students teamed up with Chinese students at Shantou University to document the emerging environmental movement in the country. The resulting multimedia project, "*China's Generation Green,*" benefited from an outsider-insider lens, and the English/Chinese-language website, published with the *Toronto Star,* won a national Edward R. Murrow Award, among other accolades (Thomson, 2014).

We spent the next several years developing this proof-of-concept further, and as the first decade of funding ran out, we reformulated the course under the name "Global Reporting Program," with global collaboration amongst students at the heart of the course's identity. The programme partners with journalism schools from around the world and also integrates subject-matter students who bring academic rigour and depth to the reporting. Partners change each year depending on the reporting topic and locations.

In 2018–19, the first formal year of the GRP, students produced *The Fish You (Don't Know You) Eat,* a multimedia and broadcast story in partnership with NBC News that traced the little-known supply chain of fishmeal from West Africa to Peru to China (Rueter, Woods, Beardmore-Gray, & Jones, 2019). The programme supported students from the U.S., Canada, Colombia, China, Brazil, India, the UK, and Uganda. This included 10 journalism students from UBC, four students from Nanjing University (China), two students from Universidad de Los Andes (Colombia), and three students from Makerere University (Uganda). In addition, our cohort included three oceans and fisheries studies students and two medical students.

The oceans and fisheries students brought a depth of knowledge to the reporting topic — they advanced the investigative reporting methods by collecting samples and specimens during fieldwork. Their field contributions led to the discovery that a fishmeal factory in Senegal was releasing effluent with toxic levels of heavy metals directly into the ocean. Their specimen collection in China also revealed juvenile fish being illegally caught to turn into fishmeal.

Journalism students from partner institutions also brought cross-cultural knowledge, language skills and regional expertise. For example, students from Nanjing University in China were able to scout locations, and brought local knowledge, as well as language skills, to the fieldwork. Ugandan students at Makerere University knew of little-publicized conflicts with illegal fishing on Lake Victoria, a topic parachute reporters likely would not have known about or been able to access.

Over the lifespan of both the IRP and GRP, students have completed 15 projects and reported from nearly 30 countries. The class has partnered with a range of media organizations, including The New York Times, The Guardian, PBS FRONTLINE, CBS News, BBC, CBC, VICE, Al Jazeera, Mongabay, the Tyee, NBC News, The World, Toronto Star, and The Globe and Mail. Student projects have also won a long list of awards, including an Emmy for Best Investigation, Online Journalism Award, Webby honour, and several Sigma Delta Chis and Edward R. Murrow awards.

Why a collaborative model?

The GRP is situated within the broader Global Reporting Centre, an independent journalism organization based at UBC whose mission is to innovate global journalism norms and practices. The programme is a place to train the next generation of global journalists and embrace that spirit of innovation and experimentation. Students have the opportunity to learn about, and critically reflect upon, the standards and practices typically used in foreign correspondence and develop new approaches. Then, they are able to put those approaches into action during their fieldwork.

For many students in the programme, this is their first opportunity to participate in fieldwork for a global production, especially of this scope and scale. So, in addition to working closely with their cross-university counterparts, students also assemble local teams who accompany them during field reporting. Reporting teams include in-country professionals, including local journalists, field producers, translators, technical professionals (videographers, photographers, etc.), security, etc. Through this collaboration, GRP students are taught ethical best practices for fieldwork, including equity, fair and prompt compensation, proper crediting and that editorial roles are clearly defined.

The GRP fieldwork component is the chance for students to take all the theories, critical reflections and techniques and apply them to practice. Often what students find is that challenging long-standing norms and practices can be difficult with such short time frames and the realities of on-the-ground reporting. This allows them to constantly refine their approach and build towards best practices within the confines, realities and limitations of timelines, budgets and media partner expectations.

The process

The GRP is governed by an independent advisory board of leading journalists and scholars. Each academic year, the board confirms a reporting topic. The topic is sent to eligible students who are then required to submit an application, which consists of a cover letter, story pitch and basic coursework and grades. To maintain independence for the instructors, the advisory board alone reviews student applications and determines admission into the programme. For global partners, local university faculty will review their students' applications and recommend admissions, which are then approved by the GRP advisory board. Global partners are not enrolled in the UBC course, but are required to earn course credits from their home institution for their participation in the programme. Each partner university has at least one assigned local faculty member who is responsible for supervising their students and administering the course on behalf of their institution.

The classroom portion of the programme is taught by leading global journalists. Each reporting team is assigned at least one faculty lead who accompanies students during fieldwork. Faculty members participate in a role similar to that of a producer. They ensure students receive guidance and support, act as a liaison between the professional team and students if/when needed and are responsible for any payments made throughout the course of the reporting trip. When appropriate and possible, the programme also includes faculty members with subject-area expertise. For example, in 2021–22, for the GRP project on ageing, the class was co-taught by UBC clinical medicine professor Dr. Videsh Kapoor with additional expert guidance from André Picard, a leading public health journalist. Go to this link to view the website: bit.ly/Ch7GRP1

Class time is divided between lecture/discussion and project prep work. For the lecture portion, students learn about issues such as othering, framing theory, ethics of working with NGOs, the correspondent-fixer relationship, alternative approaches to reporting such as "empowerment journalism" (Lefkowich, Dennison, & Klein, 2019) and remote reporting. The second portion of class involves story meetings, updates on reporting, brainstorming, collaboration with media partners, logistical preparation for fieldwork, production of the collaborative project, fact checking and rollout.

Fieldwork is planned for the December term break. This divides the course into three distinct sections: term one, reporting and pre-production; term break, fieldwork; and term two, post-production and publication. On rare occasions, if travel in December is not possible (due to visas, availability of story subjects, or other practical factors), students have travelled over the Canadian spring break period in February.

In the second semester, students follow a production schedule that is determined by the timeline, format, and deliverables set forth by their media partner(s). Since each year is different, the second semester schedule is more fluid and is often developed in collaboration with the external partners. Students are asked to complete and deliver their work to the media partner by the end of their academic year, with the acknowledgement that the project may be published at a later date depending on the media partners' schedule and priorities.

Initially GRP began as a hybrid in-person and teleconference model, with UBC-based students in the classroom, and international partner students joining online. Feedback from global students suggested that the online classes were sometimes difficult to follow — in some instances due to a lack of language skills; for others, the seminar-style class meant that online students couldn't as easily jump into conversations, which left them feeling less engaged in discussions and editorial decision-making. They were also disadvantaged by time zone differences and the general chemistry of the in-person students and instructors, which did not extend well across the teleconference screen.

The COVID-19 pandemic necessitated that GRP move online for all students. In many ways this approach created a more equal grounding. This also allowed for early class time for students on the West Coast, which provided better class time windows for many of the international students.

The GRP is a fully funded programme, supported generously by three donors (https:globalreportingprogram.org/about/#funders). The first ten years of the IRP was funded by Mindset Foundation. We then developed the GRP through pilot funding from the Jonathan Logan Family Foundation. Our current ten-year commitment for the GRP is from three donors: Mindset Foundation, The Giustra Foundation and Angus Reid Institute. All costs associated with the programme, including but not limited to, travel, transportation, visas, post-production, etc., are covered by the programme's funders. The only out-of-pocket expenses students are required to cover are necessary vaccinations and medications, any personal supplies they might need (bug nets, mosquito spray, technical clothing), travel insurance, and their meals in the field.

Reporting topics

Over the years students have covered the illegal e-waste trade, labour abuses in the seafood supply chain, access to medical morphine, the murders the Indigenous people in Brazil, illegal logging, China's emerging environmental movement, access to mental healthcare, the rise of HIV in Chile, migration stories, the fishmeal supply chain, education reforms worldwide, land grabs and global ageing.

In some years, the topic lends itself to a particular geographic location. For example, the fishmeal project naturally followed the supply chain from West Africa, to Peru, to China. In other years, the location is set, like with China's emerging environmental movement. Some of the most successful projects, however, used global geographical comparisons to examine complex issues to see how different parts of the world address challenging issues differently. This approach, with students usually broken into three different country teams, allows for a truly global project at a scale that even large newsrooms at major media outlets usually cannot achieve.

Global university partners are also chosen based on the reporting topic. Instructors reach out to universities in countries/regions where fieldwork is likely to move forward. For example, in 2021–22, for a project on ageing, students from Kyung-hee University in South Korea were well-positioned to report on the unique demographic shift underway in the country.

Challenges

There are a number of challenges to administering a global classroom like the GRP and to producing significant works of professional journalism with large international teams of students.

Class-time

Working across time zones presents a unique challenge. With more than one global university partner, there is usually no ideal class time for all students, particularly for the students who join from Asia, who often have to join class well past midnight local time. Each year, class time is re-evaluated to fit better with the timezones of partner universities, but it is difficult to accommodate all students, and this can be a barrier for some students to enroll and participate in the programme.

Academic school year

For some university partners, another barrier to participation is their academic calendar. The UBC academic calendar runs from September to April, with a holiday break at the end of December. The school year in other countries can differ quite substantially. For example, in China student semesters run from August to May, with a holiday break in January and February. Since UBC is the host university, fieldwork generally takes place during one of the UBC term breaks, which means students at partner universities are expected to make accommodations.

Further complicating matters is the fact that universities in the southern hemisphere have reversed school calendars, with their summer holiday in the middle of the course time for students in the northern hemisphere. This has made it impossible, to date, for the GRP to have students from universities south of the equator. The GRP still holds out hope, however, to integrate students from the southern hemisphere.

Global journalism norms and practices

The practice of journalism is not the same globally, which poses both challenges and opportunities. Differing norms between students around the world provide ample opportunities for cross-cultural comparisons of best practices. It also allows students to discuss different realities of press freedom across borders. The role of media partners can complicate matters, since their newsroom standards generally dominate the course's approach to a project, and this can pose difficulties for students from parts of the world who may be unfamiliar with, and even uncomfortable with, such approaches. For instance, students from countries with low press freedom like China have reported discomfort with accountability interviews, since such approaches can pose threats to local journalists. In some parts of the world, journalists have stronger political ties than in others, and this can also pose challenges, as can the practice of integrating the journalist's opinion in news copy. The standards for fact checking can also diverge across borders and oceans.

Highlighting these differing norms, without preferencing one over others, is a key part of the pedagogy of the course, and embracing those differences, while managing the expectations of media partners, is one of the challenges students must face and overcome.

Benefits

Learning opportunities

Students often remark that the GRP provided them with a professional experience that prepared them for their careers following graduation. While a publication with a media partner is not guaranteed, it is up to the students to report, pitch and ultimately secure the interest of a media organization, the GRP is a pathway for students to build a significant portfolio piece. As mentioned earlier, students have worked with a range of media organizations and their projects have won some of the top industry awards.

The fieldwork experience and team environment provide critical learning opportunities. Students learn to work in professional settings. Beyond reporting and editorial, they also learn significant production skills, budgeting, logistics, communication, pitching, etc.

Working collaboratively also helps students challenge their own assumptions and the lens they bring to their reporting. Working across cultures and disciplines opens students up to the chance to learn not just from the faculty and professionals they work with, but also from one another.

References

Lefkowich, M., Dennison, B., & Klein, P. (2019). Empowerment journalism – Commentary for special issue of Journalism Studies. Journalism Studies, *20(12)*, 1803–1809. https://doi.org/10.1080/146167 0X.2019.1638294

Plaut, S., & Klein, P. (2021). "Fixing" the journalist-fixer relationship: A critical look towards developing best practices in global reporting. In Reporting Global while being Local, 26–43. Routledge.

Rueter, A., Woods, M., Beardmore-Gray, O., & Jones, R. P. (2019). The fish you (don't know you) eat (2019). *globalreportingprogram*. Retrieved from https://globalreportingprogram.org/fishmeal/

Thomson, J. (2014). China's generation green. *UBC International Reporting Program*. Retrieved from https://globalreportingcentre.org/greenchina/

UBC School of Journalism, Writing and Media. (n.d.). *Training the next generation of student journalists*. The Global Reporting Program, University of British Columbia. Retrieved from https://globalreportingprogram.org/about/#funders

8 Student perspectives

Katherine C. Blair

Figure 8.1 Global Campus Studio Productions, Toronto Metropolitan University, Canada.

Journalism education is often characterized by experiential learning—learning by doing. This happens in any number of ways: students publishing on university websites, broadcasting to university radio stations, producing live TV programmes to a YouTube channel and going on work placements within the industry.

In my own teaching, the assignments I have set have always included the requirement for students to interview real people in the community. While all of these activities are real and intended to take students beyond university assessments into the professional world, it seems the students themselves don't necessarily see them as anything other than university assignments. When I first started involving my students in international collaborations with other university students around the world, what fascinated me was the extent to which students saw the international projects as real, beyond the other experiences they saw as being just for university.

While use of such experiential projects is common within journalism education, research into the benefits is rare. I began gathering feedback after a global project I launched in 2019 called *World Earth Day Live!* This was to be a rolling broadcast going from one university to another across the globe,

DOI: 10.4324/9781003428725-9

with stories focusing on the environment. In the end, the broadcast was abandoned as broadcast day (the fiftieth anniversary of World Earth Day—April 22, 2020) coincided with the COVID-19 pandemic which closed down our ambitious studio-based project. However, our Instagram, Facebook and X, formerly known as Twitter, platforms still carry the work that had already been completed by our partner universities.

Through that project, I heard how students had bought into the concept and its collaborative features, with one instructor telling me how upset their student had been to hear their work would not feature in that university's offering because it didn't quite meet the show's requirements. The student was devastated because although the work would still be assessed and awarded a mark, it wasn't to be part of the global production.

On another occasion, when Marion Coomey from Toronto Metropolitan University in Canada zoomed into my class as part of a session for pitching story ideas in the lead up to *Let's Talk Racism* (Global Campus Studio Productions, 2020), I witnessed my students arrive well prepared with their story ideas, and able to talk in detail about how they planned to cover them—something I'd not often seen for previous class assignments when usual excuses about not getting around to it yet were the common response. The students rose to the occasion when pressed via video communication from Marion about what they would be delivering.

A host for *Let's Talk Racism* (2020), Anna Ashitey now works at the Canadian Broadcasting Corporation (CBC) in Toronto, Canada. Ashitey (Personal communication, 2023) said it wasn't until after graduating, and starting work that she came to realize the best parts of the experience. Ashitey now works with companies in Australia, and the U.S. and appreciates the experience from her university course of learning to deal with different perspectives and different time zones. *Let's Talk Racisim* was broadcast in the months following the murder of George Floyd in the U.S.

Anna Ashitey, Canadian Broadcasting Corporation (CBC), Radio Producer

> For myself as a black Canadian, our stories are often integrated with the black African American experience. It's almost rare to hear Black Canadians or in this case someone from the Netherlands talk about what they've gone through or the history of racism, so just hearing somebody else's experience, it was eye-opening for me as a young black woman, and there was a compassion that surpassed the course. It was just a moment of hearing what someone else is going through in a way that is authentic and is safe….Despite where everyone was from, not everyone on that show was a person of colour, but everyone had a heart of compassion and a willingness to want to hear other perspectives.
>
> (Personal communication, March 9, 2023)

In November 2021, our students at Leeds Trinity University took part in a Global Campus Studio production, *Food for Thought*, hosted by students at Toronto Metropolitan University in Canada (Blair, 2022). I tasked the students in my final year TV class to produce a TV news package that related to the topic of food. Students produced a range of stories that included how food banks were being more heavily relied upon, nutrition in some food, and student cooking. Being just a participant meant the international interaction is reduced, as opposed to the host university where most of the interaction with other universities takes place. The presenters benefit from rehearsals and the recording of the programme because they see the other students, but the rest of the class are just producing content in isolation. Still for those directly involved in the international programme, they get a lot out of it. One of our presenters said it was probably the best thing she did at university.

> I loved the fact that I had interactions with people from all over the world. It was something that nobody else really gets a chance to do. It was absolutely fantastic and it was just something that I probably won't get a chance to do again.
> (Lord, A. Personal communication, 2023)

During downtime in the recording of the programme, Abbie was able to chat with one of the presenters in Toronto. They started messaging over Instagram and then eventually met up face-to-face in London.

Abbie Lord, Leeds Trinity University graduate

> We developed a love of espresso martinis and she came to London a couple of months ago and we got a chance to actually meet up together. And to this day, a year on, we still talk...if it wasn't for doing a programme like this, it gave me a chance to develop myself, not just my journalism skills, but me as a person.
> (Personal communication, April 11, 2023)

In April 2022, Leeds Trinity University volunteered to take over the Global News Relay programme, *Mind Matters*, a show focusing on mental health in the wake of the pandemic. When the host university, Hong Kong Baptist University, was unable to work from their TV studio due to COVID restrictions, my class (of 2022), which was a very talented cohort of Master of Arts (Journalism) students, took on the challenge with gusto. Not only did they come into the university on weekends to coordinate the script in pre-production, but they gave up some of their Easter holiday in order to record the programme with our international partners. In interviews, here are some responses to the experiences:

Phoebe Morton, Leeds Trinity University graduate

"I've been thinking about all the skills I got from uni. I think they all came together in the Global News Relay" (Personal communication, December 13, 2022)

Grace McGrory, BBC Radio reporter, Leeds Trinity University MA graduate

"I pushed myself out of my comfort zone and I ended up loving it. I love the presenting. I think it did definitely broaden my horizons" (Personal communication, December 13, 2022)

Georgia Levy-Collins, Leeds Trinity University graduate

"Definitely in my job now, it's helped me [being] able to think on my feet…it's given me confidence in what I'm doing and in myself" (Personal communication, December 13, 2022)

Responses to an anonymous questionnaire (Blair, 2022) back these views up with overwhelmingly positive feedback from the MA (Journalism) cohort at Leeds Trinity.

- It's been my favourite thing I've done as part of the Master's because it felt like real work rather than university work—not that university work isn't fun or useful, but it felt really inspiring and great to get to do something for a real programme and get a little glimpse into what our future careers could be like.
- What I liked best about working on Global News Relay was working as part of a team each week to create something important as well as constantly learning and bettering our skills.
- I loved being able to interact with students doing similar courses at universities across the world.

- Directing a global news show! I liked how Leeds Trinity was not only involved but hosted.
- What I liked least about working on Global News Relay was that we don't have the opportunity to do it all over again. It was one of the highlights of the course in my opinion and if I could have the opportunity to participate in more things like that I would.

In September 2022, I launched the Global Campus Studios Production, *And the Good News Is* to the students in the Netherlands, during a visit to Breda University of Applied Sciences. In an anonymous questionnaire, the overwhelming concern identified was not having enough time to get involved because the project sat outside of their assessed work. At the same time, they were also looking forward to getting involved because of the opportunity of working with other students internationally and collaborating with people all over the world.

In a follow-up interview, at the end of the project, their student TV host agreed that if the programme had been part of the course in terms of workload and marks, then it would have been more popular.

Wiktoria Pietraszek, Breda University of Applied Sciences, Netherlands

> I definitely think if we got some sort of credit for this, then, more people would also want to participate. But because we are in such a busy semester and then this is an extra thing, I think a lot of people were, 'Oh, I don't really have time to do it and I'm not getting any credit for this, so I'll pass'.
> (Personal communication, December 19, 2022)

The rehearsals brought the process to life, though.

Wiktoria Pietraszek, Breda University of Applied Sciences, Netherlands

> It just felt very professional to me compared to how our studio works here [in Breda], so I was really surprised. At the end I was like, 'Oh wow! That wasn't that bad. It was actually quite fun to do'.
> (Personal communication, December 19, 2022)

In Brazil, the programme was also voluntary and done as an extracurricular activity. Their presenter was keen to take part, unlike many of her peers.

Julya Benavide, Universidade Metodista de São Paulo, Brazil

"I'm a freshman, and many other students don't feel like it's interesting or worth it. They're like, 'oh, okay, it's just another project'. And they don't realise how cool it is to participate" (Personal communication, December 6, 2022).

Julia's enthusiasm shone through right from the start and she saw the benefits of getting involved.

Julya Benavide, Universidade Metodista de São Paulo, Brazil

"I can put it in my CV, I can put it in my portfolio, my personal portfolio. And it's a really great experience that I thought I would never have." (Personal communication, December 6, 2022).

With the programmes broadcast in English, non-English speakers were faced with a further challenge, as I found out in talking to one of the participants from Taiwan.

Vivian Chen, National Taiwan University of Sport Taichung

"For other students I think they think this is too hard for them to translate into English. I think this is hard work for the students from Taiwan" (Personal communication, December 6, 2022).

For her, the experience was worth it though.

Vivian Chen, National Taiwan University of Sport Taichung

"I want to study abroad, so I really want to have a chance to work with students from different countries, but this is not for everyone" (Personal communication, December 6, 2022).

And the international programme broadened their understanding.

Vivian Chen, National Taiwan University of Sport Taichung

> I think I learned very much from the international programmes because we only film the videos for our teacher or for our country. It's too small and we can know the things too little. So that international programme helps us a lot.
> (Personal communication, December 6, 2022)

In Toronto, where the show's concept originated with Marion Coomey, the assessment is very much focused on what is produced for the international show. That attitude drives the students from the beginning.

Taylor Scully, Toronto Metropolitan University, Canada

> "I think everyone took it really seriously right to begin with. They made sure that when they were crafting their projects, they were being really cognizant of how they were telling the story" (Personal communication, Dec 16, 2022).

Amanda Shekarchi, Toronto Metropolitan University

> I think being able to connect with people internationally was a cool opportunity for me because I think that media is very collaborative. I know some people who had taken this course [before] and they all said amazing things about it. And so just to be part of it is a bonus.
> (Personal communication, December 12, 2022)

For the students at Toronto Metropolitan University for whom the assignment formed part of their assessed work for the semester, the concerns were more varied. There were issues about the communication with the other students being virtual, confusion about the assignments, worries about the process and the skills needed, fears about workload and anxieties about communicating with students who have a different cultural background. On the flip side, like the students in the Netherlands, they were also interested in collaborating around the world, having a hands-on experience, and working on set in the TV studio. At Methodist University in São Paulo, Brazil, it was a positive experience:

Julya Benavide, Universidade Metodista de São Paulo, Brazil

> I have never seen a project with this magnitude before. So I thought, 'oh my gosh, this is really interesting and it's something that I can really work on in my future. I can put in my CV, I can put in my portfolio. And it's a really great experience that I thought I would never have. If Global Campus is happening again next year, I'm the first volunteer to participate. And definitely recommending to other students in my class because it's a really nice project.
>
> (Personal communication, December 6, 2022)

As hosts for the programme, my students at Leeds Trinity University had more at stake in the project. Two student producers and four presenters had direct contact with the seven other universities in the project prior to the broadcast, and with the rest of the class taking up studio and gallery roles during the rehearsal and the actual production, they all saw the way the programme came together as well as much of content from the other students. I was leading the project and my enthusiasm over the course of the semester must have helped frame it positively.

In an anonymous survey, many students loved it. Another said it made it the best module for him this year. Another said: it was amazing to see people all over the world in the same project doing the same thing.

Others saw it as an opportunity to learn by working out of their comfort zone. Another said that working with the other countries made him really proud of what they produced and it was a pleasure to be a part of it. Another said it prepared you more for work life, because it wasn't just an assignment for your teacher.

Students hadn't worked on a collaborative international project before, which meant it was something new to them, and pushed them outside of their comfort zone, but this had the effect of increasing their confidence. In follow-up interviews, students agreed with those who responded to the questionnaire.

Amelia Riley, Leeds Trinity University

Because I was one of the presenters, it was definitely a huge confidence booster. In first year, I wouldn't have ever opted to do this. I would have hid in the corner of the room and let someone else do it. But I think my confidence has grown over the years.

(Personal communication, December 1, 2022)

Josh Horsfield, Leeds Trinity University

I think it was good to work as part of an international project. It's always something good that you can put on your CV, definitely good for employers to see that you've been able to work on this project, as a team and with people from different countries.

(Personal communication, December 1, 2022)

Ben Rogers, Leeds Trinity University

It's a really valuable experience for me, and it's one that I'm really glad I took part in, and I'm going to take a lot away from the show that we produced, and I'm just really happy that it's something that I've been a part of, and being a presenter for the show is just a real privilege.

(Personal communication, December 1, 2022)

MJ Binns, Leeds Trinity University

"One of the things that I really enjoyed about working on the show was being able to see all the different stories that other countries had....It's amazing to see how a small crew can create something massive like this" (Personal communication, December 1, 2022).

The positive feedback, time and time again shows how worthwhile such projects are, by bringing together skills learned into one very practical project, by stretching students to acquire organizational, cultural and communication skills, and by challenging them to apply themselves to a very real exercise that forms part of their confidence boosting, and becomes an experience that moves them from student to practitioner.

References

Blair, K. (2022). Global TV projects in journalism education. *Journalism Education*, *11*(1), 42–59.

Global Campus Studio Productions. (2020). *Let's talk racism.* Retrieved from https://branched-count-6aa.notion.site/478129122d9540f0b1b218fb4ee14f67?v=c7ad\c96e978842a9932bbb11c6709c13

9 Instructor feedback

Marion Coomey

Figure 9.1

Eran Shapira, Instructor, Steve Tisch School of film and television, Tel Aviv University and Kibbutzim College of Education Technology and Art, Israel, GCS and GNR projects

"We felt like pioneers. It was like everything was new. It had the smell of something different" (Personal communication, May 1, 2023).

It takes a leap of faith to get involved in an international collaborative project. As Eran Shapira from Tel Aviv University noted, when he first got involved in Global Campus Studio Productions (GCSP) it was unlike anything he'd done before. The same is true for all of us who have taken part in these projects. As well as teaching students to be visual storytellers, training them to use equipment that's new to them and then mentoring them to produce entire

DOI: 10.4324/9781003428725-10

television programmes, we're also adding students and instructors from other countries into the mix. We're working with people from different cultures who speak a number of languages and live in very different time zones.

We interviewed instructors from several universities who have been involved in some of the projects outlined in the case studies chapters of this book.

Why get involved?

I often refer to the instructors who take part in our collaborative projects as champions. They have decided that giving their students the opportunity to work with their peers from around the world will be a positive experience, and they are fully committed to making it happen.

Sandra Whitehead, Marquette University, Madison, Wisconsin, U.S. and Rafik Hariri University Beirut, Lebanon, Pop-Up News, Global News Relay

> It's not just a matter of you telling your local story to someone internationally, but collaborating with someone who can help you tell those stories. I had students at Marquette also online while I was in Lebanon, and I always felt like the exposure for the American students was more important in many ways, because I'm in the midwest in the U.S. And they're so isolated from global things where students in Lebanon have family all over the world, and the Lebanese diaspora, and they're very tuned into European politics and American politics and world affairs much more than American students. We were looking at empathy, and did it help them empathize with people across the world. Their lives didn't intersect and you know what we found was that it gave them a beginning.
>
> (Personal communication, May 18, 2023)

Sandra Whitehead, Marquette University, Madison, Wisconsin, U.S. and Rafik Hariri University Beirut, Lebanon

> There's so much going on in the Middle East that they had access to. You know the Syrian refugee crisis, and while I was there, there was an embargo against Gaza, and you know they just had access to stories going on around them. It made them get out and meet Syrian refugees and different people that would not usually be in their sphere.
>
> (Personal communication, May 18, 2023)

Eran Shapira, Tel Aviv University, Israel

I remember very much the show about the Syrian immigrants. That was a very touching show, and was very interesting for us, as Israel is to be involved there, because it was a very different look. People that are regarded as us versus enemies. At that point it was like understanding Israeli policy. Israeli policy towards the Syrian immigrants is something that it was not easy for Israeli students to understand.

(Personal communication, May 1, 2023)

Marcelo Moreira, Professor of communication, audiovisual production, Metodista University, São Paulo, Brazil—GCS productions

The project, in addition to bringing a local view on the chosen themes, also manifests the ways of each culture in the way they produce audiovisual narratives, and in the techniques of structuring the videos. It is these experiences that serve as a starting point for me to develop more up-to-date pedagogical proposals that are in line with the practices that are being proposed by the best universities in the world to demystify the view that students from one country have about others in the areas of cultural music, food, behavior, politics.

(Personal communication, June 5, 2023)

What are the benefits?

I asked the instructors interviewed for this chapter what the benefits have been of taking part in international collaborative projects and they talked about the positive impact these projects have on their students.

Before you read what they said, I'll add that these projects benefit the instructors as well. In the many years I've produced GCSP, I've gotten to know instructors and students from all over the world. I've gained insight into their lives, their cultures, their perspectives on storytelling and their teaching methods. I've learned a lot about the many different ways university programmes are structured. In the numerous emails, phone calls and Zooms I've had with my colleagues around the world, we've all agreed how stimulating and exciting it is to have created a global community.

But first and foremost, all of us have noted how our students benefit from taking part.

Katherine Blair, Associate Professor (Professional Practice), Centre for Journalism, Leeds Trinity University, UK, GCSP and GNR

The students see these projects more than almost anything else during their time at university, as something that's real. There's a competitive aspect to delivering work that's of high quality in order to stand out to other students in other countries, and this pushes the students to engage with what they're learning in a whole new way. And for universities it's a win-win. There is no extra cost and it ticks a box for another way of internationalising the curriculum that's sustainable.

(Personal communication, May 15, 2023)

Marcelo Moreira, Metodista University, São Paulo, Brazil

"It makes an incredible difference in offering our courses, because in addition to quality theoretical and practical training, you can also offer your students an international experience in audiovisual production. This is very important for the university" (Personal communication, June 5, 2023).

Eran Shapira, Tel Aviv University, Israel

"They also want to communicate in English, because they understand the value that they can have for something like this in the future professional life, because they will have to do it" (Personal communication, May 1, 2023).

April deHaas, Former instructor, Breda University of Applied sciences, production executive of unscripted production for amazon studios, The Netherlands, GCS and GNR

The massive benefit of global collaboration with students is that you are expected, in the media, to speak English. If you are working for a major streamer or broadcaster you are expected to speak English and know how to collaborate and work across time zones. It is now more than ever, it should be mandatory for this kind of global collaboration to prepare them for what it really is.

(Personal communication, March 17, 2023)

Jenny Lam, Senior Lecturer, broadcast journalism, Hong Kong Baptist University, GCS and GNR

This is really the only chance they have as students to speak to an international audience. I have to make sure that my students understand not just speaking to a Hong Kong audience but a global audience. So this is actually a very positive experience for them. We live in just a small city. And when we've connected with people in mainland China in the north of China, for example, they need to understand that these audiences are different. So for example, they don't necessarily know what the underground train system is called. So you can't just call it the MTR because people don't know what the MTR is.

(Personal communication, May 26, 2023)

Sandra Whitehead, Marquette University and Rafik Hariri University

I always felt that there was a great benefit for American students to meet their counterparts in the Middle East, because it could dispel the stereotypes that are so strong, and so I felt the benefit was great there, but also the Lebanese thought they knew about America through the media but having the chance to talk to peers directly, internationally helps them dispel some stereotypes they had of Americans.

(Personal communication, May 18, 2023)

Cynthia Yoo, Professor of Communication, audiovisual production, Kyung-hee University, South Korea —Global Reporting Project

> My students used to have to sort of find other avenues either through student media like student radio or student newspapers on campus or other internships to get opportunities. So, taking part in the Global Reporting Program was a great experience. And I knew that at the end, they would produce a great story. So I thought this would be one of those rare opportunities. They had faith that they would produce a great piece.
>
> (Personal communication, May 28, 2023)

Sandra Whitehead, Marquette University and Rafik Hariri University

> It creates an opportunity for students who want to pursue it to develop those relationships and it gives everyone an introduction to be interested in others. And what's going on in other countries, I mean, that's what I would hope, and that's what we found that it wasn't a significant difference in their thinking, but that there was a move in the direction of being more empathetic with counterparts elsewhere.
>
> (Personal communication, May 18, 2023)

What are the challenges?

All of the instructors I spoke with said that while it is rewarding to take part in global collaborative projects, it does involve extra work.

I coordinated the Global Campus Studio Productions project for many years. I'd offer to attend classes via Zoom early in the semester to introduce myself and explain how the project works. If a class in Tel Aviv, for example, was at 9 a.m., it would be 1 a.m. for me in Toronto. I stayed up late and got up early on many occasions and my students would often volunteer to attend with me because I felt it was important for the students around the world to meet us and get excited about taking part in an international project.

Eran Shapira, Tel Aviv University, Israel

The calendar issues, the hours issues. When do we meet? I still remember the idea of transmitting a live meeting between your students and my students. And when are we going to do it? Are you coming to my lecture to meet my students? It was 1am in Toronto, and there was something there that worked very nicely and was very interesting.

(Personal communication, May 1, 20230)

Marcelo Moreira, Metodista University, São Paulo, Brazil

"It often requires work and meetings after working hours and on weekends. Any time of day or night. But the result makes up for all that effort and the feeling is always of duty done. It's gratifying" (Personal communication, June 5, 2023).

Cynthia Yoo first got involved in the Global Reporting Program as an MA student at the University of British Columbia in Canada. When she returned to South Korea and took a position at Kyung-hee University, she decided to get her students involved. But the semester dates in Canada and South Korea were very different.

Cynthia Yoo, Professor of Communication, audiovisual production, Kyung-hee University, South Korea

We produced the pieces during winter break because January and February is the winter vacation here but that's when everyone else was working on the Global Reporting Program. But I know we were always in communication, making sure that everyone knew what they had to do and everyone was motivated to do it.

(Personal communication, May 28, 2023)

That issue comes up all the time. If we produce a programme in Toronto in October, it's too early for students in the UK to take part because their semester didn't begin until late September. If we produce a programme in late

November, at the end of our semester in Toronto, it's too late for students in Australia to take part. They have already finished their semester. It involves lots of communication and negotiation between the different universities to come up with dates and times of day that work for everyone.

Sandra Whitehead, Marquette University and Rafik Hariri University

> One big issue is financial. Teachers are not paid to pursue this. We do it because we think it's a great opportunity. There's not much incentive. It's not part of your regular duties. It's something that you've added to your class, and you still have to do the rest of the class, and you can incorporate it, and they can learn from it. But there's a time commitment. So I think that for everybody wherever they are, for all the faculty it's an issue.
>
> (Personal communication, May 18, 2023)

None of the instructors I've worked with since starting GCSP in 2009 said they received any extra money or teaching credit to do the additional work involved in international projects.

Cynthia Soo-Yi told me that in South Korea, there is an itemized list of points instructors accrue and she received 0 points for taking part in the Global Reporting Project. It can also be a challenge getting funding for the costs involved in developing an international project, such as creating a website or an app, paying technical staff for overtime hours because these sorts of projects are usually not considered academic research. And sometimes the challenges come from lack of technology or facilities in some locations.

The Global Reporting Project (GRP) (Chapter 7) is a rare example of an international collaboration that is fully funded.

Sandra Whitehead, Marquette University and Rafik Hariri University

> A couple of challenges that pop in mind right away is that the electricity would turn off, and they switch to a generator every day at 5pm in Lebanon, from the Government electricity to private generator, and 5 o'clock was in the middle of class. We had no broadcast facility and no broadcast program. And so we ended up in the auditorium and I'd recruit people from different departments to help me do different things, or if students needed cameras or wanted to do something. So there's that extra administrative level of task that you're reaching out across the campus to different resources for the students.
>
> (Personal communication, May 18, 2023)

What are your final thoughts?

Over the many years I've run GCSP, some instructors have retired, some have moved to other universities or left academia, others have left the project because it was too difficult to integrate the additional work into their curriculum.

But there continue to be motivated and dedicated instructors all over the world who are passionate about taking part in a project that provides their students an opportunity to collaborate with their peers and produce news and current affairs programmes examining important issues.

Marcelo Moreira, Metodista University, São Paulo, Brazil

> With the global campus project, students understand that by producing stories about our culture, our worldview, and the reality of the society in which we live, it increases the need to tell these stories in a responsible, truthful way, legitimizing the Brazilian culture and way of being. They become more autonomous and less dependent on teachers with regard to the operation of audiovisual production equipment. In addition, they begin to have much more direct contact with the narrative production of these stories.
>
> (Personal communication, June 5, 2023)

Sandra Whitehead, Marquette University and Rafik Hariri University

> I think journalists in general appreciate the value of story and how it's the key to understanding people. And I think the same thing that you do internationally you do locally between communities and understanding people whose lives are not your own, or even understanding people in your family whose lives are not your own. I mean it's just a tool for understanding more. They got feedback from other people who are not their teachers, not their classroom peers; they get responses from other people, and which is much more like real world journalism when you put something out there in social media and somebody responds to it or questions it.
>
> (Personal communication, May 18, 2023)

Katherine Blair, Leeds Trinity University, UK

It's also heartening to see students who may not have traveled much, who may not have moved much outside their own locality, their own comfort zones, start to talk quite casually about working with students across the globe. It broadens their perspective and it not only makes what they're learning more purposeful, but also more fun.

(Personal communication, May 15. 2023)

April deHaas, Production Executive of Unscripted Production for Amazon Studios, The Netherlands, Former instructor, Breda University of Applied Sciences, —GCS and GNR

I literally work with people from all over the world in all kinds of time zones and we are collaborating on literally the biggest streaming platform in the world and we do what the students are doing and it feels seamless for me. There are no more borders. Being able to boast that they have already got experience working in an international environment creating tangible content is the key and understanding that working across time zones and cultures and different workflows and systems, and understanding others organize it that way and we do it this way.

(Personal communication, March 17, 2023)

10 Technology
Getting it right

Marion Coomey

Figure 10.1

Mark Willett Senior Media Technician Leeds Trinity University (LTU), UK

> Without realizing it, most of us 'go live' on a daily basis thanks to the recent Global Pandemic. If you think about it, you are appearing 'live' in front of a camera and mic every time you join a Teams or Zoom meeting.
>
> (Personal communication, May 15, 2023)

The early days of global collaboration

We're so used to the instant communication available on social media and our ability to send videos and images online quickly and easily that it's hard to believe that in 2000 bandwidth was limited to the extent that we couldn't send

DOI: 10.4324/9781003428725-11

videos online. When I started my first global collaborative project back then, the participating universities from around the world had to send VHS tapes in the mail in order to participate.

Professional broadcasters were using satellites to send images internationally, but the cost and lack of availability to universities made it impossible to use those technologies. And there were delays in hearing both sides of the conversation that would have made it awkward to have a live TV show with hosts in several countries.

When Global Campus Studio Productions began in 2009, we needed a way to communicate that didn't cost much money and would allow universities around the world to produce live programmes. We were producing several one-hour long current affairs shows with participants from up to 15 countries. Around that time, my colleague Rick Grunberg with the RTA School of Media at Toronto Metropolitan University (Ryerson University changed its name to Toronto Metropolitan University in 2022 due to recognition of Egerton Ryerson's participation in the Canadian indigenous residential school system) was working with a Canadian company called Haivision to develop a technology that would allow for bidirectional high definition video and many channels of audio. It was a perfect fit for our project.

Rick Grunberg, Professor, RTA School of Media, Toronto Metropolitan University, Technical Director GCSP

> It had enough channels of audio that we could integrate intercom so our control rooms could talk to each other live and we could integrate an IFB which is the earpiece, so that our producer director could speak to talent in different countries. And that box with all these audio tracks and video had very little delay.
> (Personal communication, April 4, 2023)

In other words, the Haivision technology allowed us to produce international shows with student hosts in several countries who were able to see and hear each other without pauses in the conversation. After some tests, we tried it out with one of our first streaming partners in New Zealand, and the technology worked well. The Global Campus Network (GCN) became the world's first purely internet based live production network (Head, 2011). But even with assistance from grants and a major discount provided by the manufacturer, some universities didn't have the funds to buy the technology. Then, as the project grew, new partners didn't have access to the Haivision box and some old partners dropped out. As well, some universities had technical issues, internet security features or firewalls which their IT departments were not used to dealing with and that made it difficult at times to connect the technology.

Then what?

As internet networks became faster and more reliable, we started looking for a new way to connect with each other. At that time people were starting to use Skype for personal and professional meetings. Skype developed a version that was used for broadcasters. Skype also began to develop a software version that was in the initial stages of testing. Grunberg worked with a UK company called Quicklink that made one of the first hardware components intended to connect studios for professional level interactivity. It was easy to use but it did not allow students to hear each other through earpieces and had only one channel of audio. Professional broadcasters were hesitant to use it but for the Global Campus Studio (GCSP) project, it worked well.

It's the technical staff who make all collaborative projects possible. I interviewed the people at TMU in Toronto, Canada, LTU in Leeds, UK and California State University Fresno, in the U.S. who were in charge of every technical aspect of the Global News Relay and Global Campus Studio Productions about how the technology evolved over more than two decades.

Brian Withers, Senior Production and Programming specialist with the RTA School of Media at TMU. He has run the technical side of Global Campus Studio Productions since 2009

> By the time we moved into the Skype era, video calls were a lot more commonplace and I'm sure at the other universities in our partner group as well as our own university, students were using Skype in their daily lives. The trickiest part with Skype is that we were really pushing it to its limits.
> (Personal communication, March 27, 2023)

We had frequent delays producing shows with Skype. The signal would get dropped, we would have audio and video issues and occasional difficulties connecting with some locations.

In the UK, LTU was looking for a way to produce another show celebrating World Earth Day. It was a project meant to be live for a full 24 hours.

Mark Willett, LTU, UK

> We had no platform in place at the time back then such as Zoom or Teams to hook everyone up. I had never even used Zoom before

and the Skype box felt like a no for this project. I knew I could mix our output to Livestream between the TV studio for our live sections, then suggested if every other university went live at the specified time on their own Facebook page with the links, I could screen capture that output and feed it into our live stream, thus providing a continuous 24-hour stream, mixing between our live studio and other Facebook channel content. With that technical aspect locked away in my mind, the only potential hassle with this idea was actually manning the studio for 24 hours.
(Personal communication, May 15, 2023)

For a number of years, the GCSP and GNR projects carried on using a blend of Skype, Facebook and Teams. There were ongoing technical issues but we all managed to create successful programmes.

Adapting during the pandemic

And then came the pandemic. TV studios at universities world wide were shut down. At that time, Zoom became the common method for people around the world to talk to each other. Withers at TMU said it was pretty easy to adapt.

Brian Withers, TMU, Canada

"Zoom was a pretty great fit right away because we could just put up the gallery mode in Zoom and have that be what was recorded and so each of the contributors could be on screen at the same time.
(Personal communication, March 27, 2023)

Zoom worked well but still had its technical issues.

Mark Willett, LTU, UK

"There were still audio issues, firstly internet connections – all our live productions are at the mercy of the internet connection quality at either end. Occasional freezing and stuttering is something we have no control over, especially with overseas connections" (Personal communication, May 15, 2023).

Because we weren't using our universities' TV studios and control rooms there were issues making a Zoom programme look professional. TV studios use teleprompters (also called autocues). Hosts look directly into the cameras to read their scripts. Students were able to download a teleprompter app during our Zoom shows but reading the script meant looking down at the app on their screen and not up at their laptop cameras.

And then we had to find a way for the directors of the shows to communicate with the students hosting on Zoom, to let them know when it was their turn to speak. As Withers from TMU explains, we had to use the chat room function.

Brian Withers, TMU, Canada

> If you see in the chat that your segment is coming up next, make sure you turn your camera and your mic on. I had my system set up where I was hiding all of the non video participants. So anyone in the call, as long as they didn't have their camera on, they weren't going to show up on the screen as part of the host discussion.
>
> (Personal communication, March 27, 2023)

Mark Willett, Leeds Trinity University, UK

> It was clear that whilst everyone was connected up and could communicate, my assumption that all the contributing universities would know how to feed our incoming audio directly into the presentes' earpieces was unfounded. We were feeding their output back to them due to a lack of audio mixing control at our end, thus causing an echo. It worked, somehow, and the final product looked great, but I knew everyone was not comfortable with the communication route.
>
> (Personal communication, May 15, 2023)

It took lots of practice and lots of setup and testing days to just get the participating universities to communicate with one another for us to be able to feel confident that they would be stable throughout the live production.

Brian Withers, TMU, Canada

> There was no ability for us to also do an intercom channel where we could hear, or the other schools could hear, our show director.. And people would get dropped out and then, of course, you couldn't just rejoin the call kind in the background. Somebody would have to stop and click, accept, and answer the phone call. Zoom doesn't love people talking over one another. It takes the primary voice, and it brings the level down on everything else, and that to me is not really in line with what it's like in a broadcast situation.
>
> (Personal communication, March 27, 2023)

Ongoing challenges

Because it was difficult for the directors and hosts in the different locations to hear each other, I'd often open a separate Zoom or Skype link and type in the cues, letting each location know when it was their turn to be on camera. It was a good test of my typing skills as I'd be constantly writing: "5 seconds to Brazil. Cue Brazil", "Cue Israel", "Go to Taiwan for a response to Israel," etc.

One year, my students took part in the Global News Relay project and nothing was working in our studio. We couldn't see or hear the people in the other locations. The show was airing live so we had to do something. Withers explains how we solved that problem.

Brian Withers, TMU, Canada

> Okay, let's try plan C, let's try plan D, and then I think we finally got to the point where we were at risk of losing the whole day. You take into consideration the time zones that all of our other partner schools are in and ultimately make the decision to go live without having our cutaway angles and our 2 shots.
>
> (Personal communication, March 27, 2023)

I ran into our studio in Toronto with my laptop and made a connection over Wi-Fi. It didn't look professional having my students crunched together looking down at a small laptop screen but it allowed us to take part in the live programme.

On some occasions during the Zoom shows producing during COVID-19, there were issues with students who had poor internet quality from home.

Terry Dolph, Chief Engineer, Media, Communications and Journalism Dept., CSU Fresno, California, U.S.

> And so that was always a big worry to make sure that we had all the feeds working, because sometimes the internet gets clogged down the line. From here to Canada or something or across to Asia, you're going to have internet problems because there's so many switches and passes like the freeways going. You get traffic slow down, because there's other traffic on it, too. So you just have to make sure you have a steady, reliable, fast Ethernet internet connection.
> (Personal Communication, April 10, 2023)

One solution was to stop doing the shows live. During COVID we started recording the shows so we were able to pause and make corrections when there were technical problems. We'd record all the hosted parts and then edit them together before putting it on Facebook, YouTube and our websites.

Learning curve for students

The professionals like Withers, Willett and Dolph all have decades of professional broadcast experience, and they still face challenges. Imagine what the learning curve is like for the students.

Brian Withers, TMU, Canada

> You're asking the students to do all this, and they've never done this before, and so even a student who's edited and used Premiere and has cut lots of things and maybe they've even worked in news or the live production type of space, it's unlikely that they've done an edit before where they've got to put together an entire show.
> (Personal communication, March 27, 2023)

Students have to be reminded that when they use their laptops they need to frame the shot using the techniques they've learned in class: put a couple books under your laptop to get the camera up to eye level, or make sure you're not sitting in a room where all the light is behind you, and we can't see your face at all.

Mark Willett, LTU, UK

Give your webcam a good cleaning, avoid having a window right behind you, frame yourself nicely on the screen using the rule of thirds, and more importantly for audio quality – wear a headset, earphones or earpods. It makes a world of difference to the audio quality.
(Personal communication, May 15, 2023)

When you're working with students from around the world, it's not just our spoken languages that are different, so are our technical languages.

Brian Withers, TMU, Canada

For example, we call the switch that switches camera sources a video switcher here, but other places in the world call it a vision mixer. So some of the terminology that we use in Canada is not universally used, and working with the different tech folks at all of our partner schools I find myself googling 'what do they call this in Brazil?'
(Personal communication, March 27, 2023)

What's next?

There continue to be developments that make the technical side of international collaborations easier. As noted, one of the biggest challenges in producing collaborative programmes is communication between the people in the control rooms around the world and the students who are hosting the shows. On a few occasions, we used an intercom app that we distributed to our international partners. But we didn't continue using it because the students who were hosting the programmes from their laptops found it difficult to pay attention to hosting and to the intercom technology at the same time.

Brian Withers, TMU, Canada

You know. Sit up straight. Look at the camera. Be a good presenter, while also having to worry about the challenge of using the intercom app. And then you've got one earbud, which is your co-host, and then you've got the other earbud, which is your control room cueing you.
(Personal communication, March 27, 2023)

Many of the countries involved in our collaborative shows do not speak English as their first language. At those universities, the videos and interviews produced by the students can include subtitles. But the hosting has always been done in English. It's now possible because of advances made through AI to do live, instant translation in multiple languages. Our projects have not yet experimented with automatic subtitles or automatic translation but hope to in the near future.

Some broadcast technologies have options like Zoom interconnected within their systems.

Brian Withers, TMU, Canada

We take a zoom call and convert the video signal out of the laptop to an SDI (Serial Digital Interface) video signal. We can feed it into our multi-camera switcher, and use that essentially the same as one of our camera sources within our own studio. And so we really have moved into this hybrid environment where we can be much more flexible, based on what our partners have available.

(Personal communication, March 27, 2023)

Some of our partners have full production studios but others do not. We've had universities set up in classrooms, libraries, auditoriums and conference rooms. It's become more and more possible to just find a quiet room and connect to other partners around the world.

Last words

Terry Dolph, Chief Engineer, Media, Communications and Journalism Dept., CSU Fresno, California, U.S.

Articulating with other universities across the world is very exciting and interesting because you get a different perspective. You get to see what other people are doing, too. So you can adjust your program, and maybe you pick up something that you like from one of the other colleges. You can incorporate it into your plan. It's very exciting for students, technicians and faculty. I think it is a great opportunity to learn coordination on a global scale.

(Personal communication, April 10, 2023)

Table 10.1 Check-list: What you need to know to set up your own collaborative project

Connect well in advance with each partner	Get an understanding of their setup What earpieces do they have? Where is your signal going?
Do you need any additional equipment?	What wires and cables do you need?
Do technical tests	Schedule test times with your partners around the same time of day, when the productions are going to take place. If it was a particularly heavy day with internet usage you'll know, if that was going to be the most available bandwidth between your partners.
Make sure there's a strong audio connection between control rooms.	Can the hosts hear each other? Can the people in the control room hear each other?
Who is speaking?	Make sure there are only a few people in the control room speaking at the same time. Make it clear to the student hosts and the people behind the scenes when they should mute their microphones.
Have a plan B	If the tape doesn't roll or the audio isn't working or someone on camera has missed a cue, what will you do to keep the show going? Whether a show is live or recorded, take some time at the end to redo hosted segments that were awkward or contained a lot of mistakes.
Post production	Make sure you record the show! If the show is not live, make sure you have students available to edit (to put in graphics and titles). Does everyone know where everything is? Good file management is crucial. I recommend setting up a folder on Google Drive. Put all of the videos and graphics and images and scripts required for the show in that one location. Make the files available to everyone involved in the show.

References

Head, S. K. (2011). Canada: University unveils the CNN of universities. *University World News Africa Edition*. Retrieved from https://www.universityworldnews.com/post.php?story=20110716144422487

11 The challenges of an uneven playing field

Sylvia Vollenhoven

Figure 11.1 University of Johannesburg, South Africa.

Introduction

It is one of the coldest days of the year. In winter, the Johannesburg temperatures often dip below freezing. Central heating is a luxury beyond the means of almost everyone. The lecture room is a studio with the powerful ceiling spotlights turned on for warmth. Busi, one of the students from the rural areas, tells the class she has been eating a watery maize porridge for weeks because she has no money for food. Cold and hungry in the richest city in Africa.

When her story has been told, we are not sure how to switch gears and turn our attention to a class on filmmaking. I have learned as a media professional that navigating the tricky terrain of empathy does not mean rushing headlong towards a solution. Today, Busi is asking us just to listen.

The University of Johannesburg (UJ)

The way students say it, the abbreviation UJ has an offbeat ring to it. Next to our more established counterparts like Wits or UCT, the acronym has developed a working-class cachet. The defensive rebelliousness of the UJ students spills over onto competitive social media with memes. One Facebook image has a smartly dressed young woman eating out but looking crestfallen. The caption says, "When he takes you out to dinner but you find out he goes to UJ."

Wits or the University of the Witwatersrand has the deep economic divisions embedded symbolically in its name. The name is Afrikaans for White Water Ridge, a reference to the rivers and waterfalls that flow from the ridge or continental divide. The University of Cape Town (UCT) sits high on a hill side-by-side with a contested colonial monument overlooking the sprawling Black townships where few young people can afford its fees.

Coming down to earth in recent times, UJ has become the most comfortable home for students and staff who prize a decolonial and proudly African ethos. With its roots firmly in apartheid soil, UJ is a microcosm for modern South Africa. (UJ was established in 2006 when the all-white Rand Afrikaans University or RAU merged with two other tertiary establishments.) The student population of more than 50,000 comes mainly from working class and lower middle-class Black families from across the region and beyond. A succession of visionary African academics has contributed to UJ developing its own character and ethos in a relatively short time. I have worked at several South African universities as well as one in Britain. UJ manages to achieve what few others offer. There is a sustained and determined effort to place Africans and Africanism at the centre of their scholarship.

When Busi tells her story, there are several unwritten codes related to African cultural imperatives that support her. She has enough faith in these pillars to share her experience. The UJ zeitgeist is like an added bolster. Sometimes these things are discussed; sometimes they are wordless.

Beyond the campus, the university finds itself in the richest city of one of the most unequal nations in the world. This has a more profound effect on students than the North/South Divide. A World Bank report released in March 2023 finds that the Southern African Customs Union (SACU) is the most unequal region in the world with South Africa having distinctly higher inequality than the rest (Galal, 2023)

Taking an aerial view of Johannesburg, you will see a Central Business District that has become like a dystopian nightmare. In the '90s as a foreign correspondent, I lived at a five-star hotel on Main Street. Now it is boarded up and surrounded by rubble that is no longer collected. To the west sits UJ on a road that starts out as Empire and then becomes Kingsway. Close by is a mining belt that once provided half of the world's gold. To the south is the renowned Soweto township bordered by mine dumps. To the east, once middle-class neighbourhoods battle the encroachment of the collapse of the CBD. And, finally in the north is a concentration of obscenely rich suburbs and business districts that have become the refuge of those fleeing the chaos of a failing state.

The students I teach come from all over South Africa—fewer than 10% from the rest of the continent and further abroad—to navigate this African city of more than six million people with its seemingly insurmountable problems.

The theme

The fourth-year honours students who participate in the Global Campus Studio Productions (GCSP) and the Global News Relay (GNR) projects are from both the Applied Journalism as well as Film and Television modules. It is only at the fourth-year level that we combine these applied classes to engage in practical work. The class is capped at 30 students split evenly between the two disciplines. By the time students reach their fourth year, there is a buzz of anticipation around the special projects. They speak excitedly about the thrill of being connected with students from around the world who are all addressing the same themes.

Working in groups of about seven or eight students, they are assigned roles related to the production of short documentaries. Each group functions as a film crew tackling the full film value chain from conception to distribution.

Every year, when we participate in GCS or GNR, we discuss the themes and invariably adapt them to suit the South African reality. For example, a GCS theme called *The Good News Is* containing positive local news stories became *The Speech of Freedom* for the UJ students. They adapted the global theme against the backdrop of 2019 being the International Year of Indigenous Languages and searched for innovations in urban expression that point the way to a more inclusive, more tolerant future. The clothes we wear, the fashions that we embrace and the décor of our spaces all speak a distinct language. These are stories of urban self-expression and language that are breaking boundaries.

Two of the best films inspired by this theme were *Fragmented* and *Painting Hope*. The former tells the story of Neo, whose name means gift. They grew up in a place called Alexandra Township under great pressure from society to conform but Neo defied convention and started dressing as a woman, while embracing a career in fine arts that helped to express a fluid gender identity. Go to this link to view his story: bit.ly/Ch11UJ1

Painting Hope is about an artist called Tony who experienced the wake-up call of a near fatal car accident. It forced him to turn his life around, and this talented young man now has a unique graffiti-style clothing brand, while also sharing his skills with young people. Go to this link to view his story: bit.ly/Ch11UJ2

Then came the harsh realities of lockdown. We turned our attention to telling stories about the effect of the COVID-19 pandemic on our lives. As isolation, depression and the full impact of online classes took its toll, it often became almost impossible to keep the work on track.

I have to pick the students whose stories I tell here very carefully. One student dropped off the radar. He was a top student but was suddenly not present in the online classes and was not submitting assignments. When I finally managed to talk with him, his explanation left me at a loss. He is from Zambia. Back home, a favourite uncle died followed shortly after by one of his grandmothers. His younger brother, a fellow student on campus, looked to him for guidance and support. But he started drinking and contemplating either dropping out and going home or getting sucked further into this new reality in a tough city. I suggested he write a film script using his uphill battle as inspiration. For a while, it worked, and a promising script developed. But then he disappeared and returned to Malawi. Before he left, he sent me a letter from his doctor testifying to a stint in hospital for depression.

There are rudimentary counselling services on campus, but the students have a host of reasons for not always using them. A simple problem is that the entrance to UJ PsyCad (Centre for Psychological Services and Career Development) is around the corner from the film studio where they have their lectures and do their post-production. It is too risky to be seen going there. Understanding and empathy for psychological problems have not increased despite the pressures of the pandemic. In addition, PsyCad does not provide specialist therapy.

One student who gave PsyCad a wide berth was the usually irrepressible Fani. Her qualities made her the undisputed leader of any group in which she found herself. But then the hostels had to be cleared. Fani logged onto lessons from home where her family, inquisitive younger kids and interfering older relatives, constantly took turns to say hello to the professor. But that was on a good day. She sent a message to say she could not keep up with her cell phone. UJ sent her and many other students laptops on loan. The next message said there was no money for data. We sent her a USB dongle with data loaded. But Fani was still defeated because South Africa's electricity supplier, Eskom, introduced rolling blackouts. The cell towers are mostly down when the power is cut. People in Fani's area connect to Eskom's power supply illegally, dodging the steep bills. By way of punishment, the power to her area gets cut completely for days on end.

I feel there should be way more than gown, mortar board and certificate for students like Fani when they graduate.

Despite it all, they produce and edit a show for the Global Campus Studio about how the pandemic has affected their lives. Not all of their stories make it into the lineup for the international collaboration.

The following year when the pandemic was once again the focus, the theme for the GNR show was *Transformed*. Two of the best films are *The Business of Dying* and *Under Pressure*. As always they don't have to look too far for their stories.

The Business of Dying is the story of the stepfather of one of the students, Khanyi Xayimpi. Jabu Pasha starts a photography business but all his equipment is stolen. The day after gangsters clean him out, they return to rob him of his pick-up van as well. Subsequently he lands a job at the national carrier South African Airways (SAA). But the pandemic forces SAA to sack Pasha and many other workers. In a desperate bid to save his family from losing their home he starts a funeral business.

Despite the student crew being less than half his age and the friends of his daughter, Pasha breaks down on camera as he recounts the trauma of the recent past. For the young filmmakers capturing the account of his ordeal is an invaluable experience.

Under Pressure is the story of one of their fellow students. Simphiwe joins a group of university students who provides online tutorials for matric (final high school year) learners. Despite being overwhelmed by her own work and having to cope with the new challenge of distance learning, the young people she tutors score top marks.

When Global Campus Studio Productions focuses on the theme of language, the UJ students interpret it as *Lost In Translation*. Their films focus on the power of language and how meaning is sometimes lost, changed or compromised.

In *Ung'Shoote* (shoot me) Sabelo Khumalo, an aspiring student artist and orphan, finds solace in the vibrant Amapiano genre of South African music. But his favourite song triggers painful memories for his beloved Grandmother, taking her back to the violence of apartheid.

All their stories are close to home; *Misery Loves Company* is the story of James, a student in the class. After a romance ends, James is heartbroken. He goes on a date with the enigmatic Molly and they have sex. But somewhere in a drunken encounter there has been miscommunication and Molly ghosts him afterward, leading James to fear that he raped her.

Sometimes they are hesitant to tell their stories but always it is deeply personal and they are not afraid of exploring painful situations.

Challenges and benefits

From conversations with colleagues at universities around the world, I get the impression that foreigners expect an African University to struggle with technology. On the contrary, the UJ studios and lecture rooms have state of the art equipment. The students, like young people everywhere, have no problem staying abreast of developments. I have to be mindful that with the more technical aspects of filmmaking they are sometimes way ahead of me.

But when most of them go home, it is another world. For most of the students, the difference between the resources on campuses and their domestic reality is vast. One young man, who has come from a university in another province, tells me the main reason he has chosen UJ is because it is far away from an alcoholic and abusive mother.

The reality of their lives and of the world out there is one of the biggest challenges when they are shooting their films. The university cannot always provide them with funds and transport to get to their locations. So, almost every year, they do informal crowd funding for the necessary resources.

In addition to this hurdle, they cannot keep the equipment overnight or use it on weekends. Often they shoot in highly dangerous surroundings without any form of security. Johannesburg has the second highest crime index on the African continent (Galal, 2023). It is not uncommon for professional crews with hired security guards to lose their equipment. In one incident, a senior SABC TV news reporter, Vuyo Mvoko, was robbed live at gunpoint on air (SABC TV, 2015).

In South Africa, rolling electricity blackouts have become part of our daily reality. In the Gauteng province where UJ is located, the water is often shut down in addition to the hours of daily power cuts. This plays havoc with even the best production schedule.

The films the students produce are part of their course work and count towards their year mark. The marks are split between the pre-production process, the production and editing. They work in groups and are assessed according to the collective effort as well as their individual roles. Anonymous peer reviews ensure that students evaluate each other's efforts as well, positively or negatively.

To give them the extra skills needed and to boost their confidence the university has a special budget for independent industry professionals to do master classes and what we call the annual Global Campus Boot Camp. These are opportunities for intense upskilling in specialist areas.

When the production and post-production process becomes intense, the film and television lecturers working with them on the Global Campus films have to tread carefully. Their passion for this kind of storytelling sometimes causes them to neglect the demands of their other modules, especially the more theoretical ones.

The biggest challenges include ensuring the safety of the students, providing them with the resources they need to shoot on location, and providing them with a learning environment that is mindful of the demands of their personal circumstances. During COVID, I often felt that it was somehow ironic that we were imposing these strict measures on students who had to brave the streets of Johannesburg every day without protection.

When a student is hungry, struggling financially or unsafe and/or unsupported at home the teaching and learning environment should take cognisance of this without singling people out for the embarrassment of charity handouts. After listening to Busi's story we made sure that we redirected some of the funds available for the project we were working on so that there could be basic daily snacks for everyone. We also ensured that we spoke with some students confidentially so that we could raise funds for their transport to and from UJ every day.

As an international group, we should explore funding sources for the Global Campus Studio Productions and Global News Relay projects that will enable:

- Students working in hostile off campus environments to be more protected.
- Struggling students to have access to micro grants for their daily needs.

The benefits of the projects are many. The most important one is the experience of working with their international peers. The isolation of apartheid has affected all South Africans. We have still not recovered from that feeling of being cut off from the rest of the world and not being fully integrated into the African continent.

For almost every young person participating in the project, this is their first encounter with students from countries outside of Africa, especially from the global north. It gives them a special sense of pride to see their stories competing very well with those from their counterparts elsewhere. The world is not a welcoming place for a young African. This international experience helps them see at a very basic level how they compare with students in countries where there are less socio economic problems and more material resources.

However, during classroom discussions, we have often contemplated the downside of too much affluence and how it impacts negatively on creativity and resourcefulness.

What's next

At UJ we are looking forward to developing this relationship so that it becomes an even more significant platform for growth and collaboration. We should explore jointly how we make this project a safe and generous space where the inequality of the world is minimised.

The experience with the GCSP and GNR has resulted in UJ exploring collaboration closer to home. As a result, we are now benefiting from the experience honours graduates gain on this project for a post-graduate initiative. The best Global Campus films are given accolades at the annual UJ Flare Awards. The prizes are internships on a project Called *Stream Learn*. This is a collaboration between UJ, the national broadcaster SABC, the National Film & Video Foundation and the Gauteng Film Commission.

The interns are recently graduated honours students (winners of the Flare Awards). We team them up with professional filmmakers who assist them with producing content for SABC Education. The premise of StreamLearn is that the professionals give them a series of hands-on master classes. These sessions are filmed and turned into video tutorials about the basics of filmmaking. So while they are still learning about the industry themselves, they are teaching others.

Peer to peer education with a real income and tangible benefits. They also have a valuable industry calling card by way of their credits on an educational series that is broadcast terrestrially and online.

References

Galal, S. (2023). Cities with the highest crime index in Africa in 2023. *Statista*. Retrieved from https://www.statista.com/statistics/1328901/cities-with-highest-crime-index-in-africa/#:~:text=In%202022%2C%20Pretoria%20(South%20Africa,of%20roughly%202082%20index%20points

SABC News. (2015). *SABC News crew robbed at gunpoint*. YouTube. Retrieved from https://www.youtube.com/watch?v=u369A8Y2IF8

12 Industry

How the pros do it

Faith Sidlow and Katherine C. Blair

Figure 12.1

Previous chapters have looked at how collaboration is being used in journalism and media education. Ultimately, the goal of higher education courses is to equip students for life after graduation, and in journalism, that usually means a job. The collaborative nature of these international projects may seem at odds with the competitive nature of professional journalism.

In this chapter, we will examine professional journalists' best practices on the international desk and how they collaborate with foreign news agencies and freelancers in the context of international news coverage.

The changing landscape of journalism

There has been a profound shift in the journalism landscape. The digital revolution coupled with the proliferation of social media has disrupted traditional media models and challenged the financial stability of many news organizations. While many of these organizations are slow to adapt, some have begun to reach out to form collaborative partnerships with other media outlets.

DOI: 10.4324/9781003428725-13

One example is a public radio station in Boston, Massachusetts. Victor Hernandez, chief content officer at WBUR, is the former director of coverage for CNN U.S., where he was responsible for a 50-person national desk at global headquarters.

Now at WBUR, he oversees two national news programs and works collaboratively with other media outlets such as the Futuro Media Group, dedicated to diversity reporting; The Trace, focused on reporting on gun violence; The Grist, which is dedicated to environmental reporting, as well as the BBC; CNN and the Washington Post.

Victor Hernandez, Chief content officer WBUR public radio; Former director of coverage for CNN US

> The Washington Post saw us as the perfect partner because they were going to reach an entirely new type of audience. And we saw value in that because they're the Washington Post and they have breaking news, not just here in the U.S. but around the world.
> (Personal communication, June 14, 2023)

Hernandez said collaborative projects are complicated, require intense coordination and are never entered into for convenience or efficiency.

Victor Hernandez, Chief content officer WBUR public radio; Former director of coverage for CNN US

> Partnerships are 10 times harder than if we just decided to do a thing ourselves. They never make life easier. The coordination, the communication, the legalities, the who's responsible for what? Who's on the hook for what? Who's paying for what? Who's benefiting from what? Where do we point people? To your properties or our properties? What does an equitable divide look like? It is so complex. But when you strike gold and you find the ideal partner and the blend of what they bring and what we bring meets so wonderfully in the middle, it makes it all worth it.
> (Personal communication, June 14, 2023)

Hernandez said as difficult as these collaborations are, they also bring about some of the best reporting, and that's why his public radio station continues to partner with other news organizations.

On an international level, the Qatari state-owned Arabic language network contracts with hundreds of freelancers around the world, who submit daily logs with story ideas.

David Poort, International desk editor, Al Jazeera English

> If you're on a news desk in Doha, you see these logs trickling in the whole day. And then people like myself, news editors, keep a close eye on that and make sure to filter out the good stuff—stuff that we can actually use in our broadcast. Not only the newsworthy stuff, but also the more interesting nuggets that bring some color to the broadcast.
>
> (Personal communication, July 18, 2023)

To say these freelance jobs are highly sought after is an understatement. A recent post by an Al Jazeera editor on the social media platform X, formerly known as Twitter, generated 127,600 views and 498 retweets. The post simply said, "I'm looking for freelancers from Kenya, South Africa and all of Lusophone, Africa. If you report or write on culture, conflict, social justice, please email me" (Egbejule, 2023).

However, Poort said the foreign correspondents are Al Jazeera's bread and butter because they are the journalists who fill the broadcasts on a daily basis.

"Al Jazeera would be absolutely nothing without its correspondents around the world," Poort said.

Tim Singleton, head of international news at Sky News in the UK, said their network recognizes that a conventional TV product is not the first thing that most people are going to consume on a story.

Tim Singleton, Head of international news at Sky News, London, UK

> It's likely to be on a mobile platform. It's going to come on our app, preferably, but we have to accept also that there are other platforms not owned and operated by us where our products are going to appear. This year it happens to be TikTok. We've got exponential growth in our TikTok products.
>
> (Personal communication, January 22, 2023)

The cost of doing news

Singleton said Sky News, like other news organizations, has issues with the inability to monetize content on social media platforms because "the audience isn't guaranteed."

In response to budgets being tightened, coupled with the changing technology, journalists and producers are having to do more with less.

Stephanie Jenzer, a senior producer based in London with the Canadian Broadcasting Corporation, said she has seen many changes over the three decades she's been working for the CBC. Back then, "we had more people in major capitals dedicated to filing for our 24-hour news network. And that doesn't really exist anymore. We have more freelancers, more stringers filing from different parts of the world" (personal communication, April 10, 2023).

Elizabeth Palmer, a foreign correspondent for CBS, said editorial decisions are driven by costs.

"As news production is getting more expensive, companies like CBS are just shutting down their foreign bureaus," Palmer said. "It's a steady melting away of having dedicated foreign correspondents in important places" (Personal communication, May 15, 2023).

CBC still has foreign bureaus in Washington, London and the Middle East. Its bureaus in Moscow and China are gone. Only two people, a correspondent and cameraman/editor/producer, remain in their "pocket bureau" in India.

CNN still operates 25 international news bureaus on six continents. Video is fed to CNN's news service, CNN International Newsource, which distributes video, live events and interviews to 200 international and 850 domestic affiliates in the U.S. (CNN Worldwide Fact Sheet). But CNN has also shuttered many of its bureaus.

Appetite for news

Former director of coverage for CNN, Hernandez, said American apathy is partly to blame.

Victor Hernandez, Chief content officer WBUR public radio; Former director of coverage for CNN US

> I think it is a subject for a lot of American audiences that believe in the nobility and believe in the altruistic benefit of what international news coverage, awareness, and consumption could offer. But I don't think enough people actually show up for that to sustain it.
>
> (Personal communication, June 14, 2023)

But when world events take place such as the war in Ukraine or unrest in Pakistan or Israel, interest in global affairs spikes, and that's when freelancers on the ground become crucial.

Elise Labott, founder/editor-in-chief, Zivvy News; former CNN global affairs correspondent

> If there is a place where we don't have a bureau, you need to work with a cameraman or a stringer or a fixer. And if you need to find a feed point or a studio where you can report from live—CNN had a lot of bureaus around the world but we didn't have it in every country—so often it was using freelance employees, and most of them are very good.
> (Personal communication, July 14, 2023)

While many broadcast networks are closing bureaus, digital organizations are expanding. The Washington Post added 15 new international positions in 2023 with 26 news bureaus around the world (Washington Post PR, 2023).

The New York Times operates 30 international bureaus with 200 journalists (The New York Times, 2021a), and as many as 1,700 New York Times journalists travel the world to report on international news from 160 countries (The New York Times, 2021b).

The 24/7 news cycle

Technology is the biggest challenge. Where satellite feeds were required to transmit stories, almost everything is filed through the internet. Correspondents can work more quickly, but the workload has increased with the perceived need to feed social media platforms with content on top of content.

Couple that increased workload with a nine-hour time difference for Labott, the requirement to report all day in the time zone you're in, then report for the newscasts in the U.S. and then report again on the ground the next day, and the pressure becomes insurmountable. Labott, who covered stories in the Middle East for CNN, said she learned to adapt to time zones with little or no sleep.

Elise Labott, founder/editor-in-chief, Zivvy News; former CNN global affairs correspondent

> I remember this one time in Pakistan in 2007, when Benazir Bhutto came back for the first time, we were staying up all night, maybe

getting like 15 to 20 minutes of sleep between live shots and then have to go back and do another live shot and then report on the ground all day long. The only way you can really do it is not get any sleep, and it was really, really difficult.

(Personal communication, July 14, 2023)

There has been a shift in audiences who are now more able to access news from more places in the world, far from where they're based. This has meant that the traditional national broadcaster no longer has just a national audience. The audience can be based anywhere.

Tim Singleton, head of international news at Sky News, London, UK

The challenge is using technology and all the new things at our disposal to meet audiences where those audiences are in a global sense. Traditionally, a UK broadcaster would be looking at a UK audience, but the availability of platforms like YouTube, Twitter, TikTok etc. means that our work is now being disseminated to a much bigger pool of potential viewers and readers.

(Personal communication, January 22, 2023)

Singleton said there are issues about monetizing those new areas so that they contribute to the business model, but that also means the audience for Sky News is now global. There are now more 24-hour news networks than ever before: CNN, BBC, Al Jazeera, China Global Television Network (CGTN).

Global news for a global audience

Executive news producer George Alexander, who works for the state-run China news network CGTN, said their coverage of the news extends far beyond the borders of China to North and South America and even Cuba.

George Alexander, executive news producer, CGTN

We'll decide what we're doing based on 'Here's what Europe's doing; here's what Africa's doing, and here's what Beijing is doing.' We have four hubs, and we follow the sun, covering what's happening. And then, something happens, and everyone goes there. Turkey [and its earthquake] would be an example.

(Personal communication, March 9, 2023)

Access to so much news around the world means that people can make their own decisions about events. Alexander said people need to see what's been said in more than just their own country.

A global audience means there are more challenges in delivering news because the audience is expanding.

"It's about how we choose our stories and adapt to that whilst still remaining relevant to the core UK audience," Singleton said.

Singleton said there are new audiences beyond the UK who are sampling the news.

"For example, on the Ukraine war on the YouTube platform, there's a massive audience in America—big, big numbers for some of our graphic explainers—about what's happening in Ukraine," Singleton said.

Collaborating to get the story

One key driving force behind the rise of collaboration is the recognition that no single news organization or journalist can comprehensively cover all aspects of a complex story. In that way, collaboration enables pooling of resources, access to diverse perspectives, and the ability to tackle stories from multiple angles. By working together, journalists can uncover hidden truths, provide context, and produce nuanced and impactful reporting.

For Al Jazeera, actually collaborating with other news organizations is rare.

David Poort, international desk editor, Al Jazeera English

> You see, we're all journalists. We're competitive and we want to have it first and have it right. I'm not sure if a collaborative thing like you mentioned would work in a professional setting. Obviously, we at times have shared sources or news stories, and we sometimes also participate in these content sharing deals when it comes to really big investigations, like we did with WikiLeaks. But when it comes to regular news, I don't think we're very good at sharing as journalists.
> (Personal communication, July 18, 2023)

The Panama Papers in 2016 was a groundbreaking investigation led by the International Consortium of Investigative Journalists (ICIJ) involving the collaboration of over 370 journalists in 80 countries from more than 100 media organizations worldwide. The project exposed a vast network of offshore tax havens and the use of shell companies for money laundering and tax evasion.

The collaborative effort resulted in the publication of numerous stories, revealing the involvement of prominent individuals and sparking global conversations about financial secrecy

And there have been other examples such as The Paradise Papers in 2017, again spearheaded by the ICIJ, and coverage of the climate crisis. These examples demonstrate how collaboration in journalism has been instrumental in unraveling complex stories, holding power to account and amplifying the impact of investigative reporting. Through shared resources, expertise, and a commitment to journalism, collaboration has proven to be a powerful tool in uncovering hidden truths and driving social change.

In this context, collaboration has emerged as a strategic response to the challenges faced by the industry. Sometimes it is individual journalists and producers helping each other out in the field rather than an organized campaign of investigation.

Jenzer of the CBC experienced this type of cooperation when she was in the Jerusalem, Middle East bureau, where she would go out on shoots with her colleagues at the Australian Broadcasting Corporation.

Stephanie Jenzer, Senior News Producer, Canadian Broadcasting Corporation

> I can remember when I went to Myanmar a number of years back, working with a correspondent of a major American paper. We weren't competing against each other, but in that authoritarian environment, we were in the same group. We travelled under the auspices of a government tour. I'm not sure if collaboration is the right word, but certainly cooperation when we could. But this kind of thing happens pretty informally depending on where you are in the world; what the story is.
>
> (Personal communication, April 10, 2023)

Jenzer said sometimes it is safer to stick together and share information in a dangerous situation. When that happens, she uses local journalists, producers or fixers from the region, who have their own networks on the ground.

While collaboration arrangements are not formally entered into, they often share information on WhatsApp groups.

Stephanie Jenzer, Senior News Producer, Canadian Broadcasting Corporation

This exists in Ukraine. They are somewhat affiliated with Ukrainian official sources, so it's just a good one-stop-shop to ask if someone is going from A to B and is there a free space in a vehicle, to exchanging information on what's going on in a certain part of Ukraine militarily. In Turkey during the recent earthquake, there was a WhatsApp group for local journalists who came to cover the earthquake.

(Personal communication, April 10, 2023)

Jenzer said she sees this type of collaboration continuing alongside the use of Telegram channels.

CBS makes use of freelancers in a range of capacities, but stories are still usually fronted by a CBS reporter. When a story happens unexpectedly and there isn't a CBS reporter on the ground, they often use a BBC reporter.

"I think for CBS, they have a quality control, a standard, and they will want to have control over everything from the production details to the delivery of the correspondent," Palmer said.

Collaboration also extends beyond the boundaries of traditional news organizations. It has opened opportunities for journalists to engage directly with their audiences, leveraging the knowledge, insights and experiences of citizen journalists and subject matter experts.

Collaboration can range from formal partnerships between news organizations to ad hoc collaborations between individual journalists. At CGTN, journalists at the scene are used as guests or contributors.

"If you're there in Turkey on the spot, we'll say he's a journalist or she's a journalist, but that's besides the point. The idea is they're there and they're telling us what's happening," Alexander said.

At CBS, it is a different story.

If you're CBS and you see the demand for news dwindling, or in any legacy news company, as management you'd have to be asking if it's worth the effort of trying to commission and train and corral all sorts of disparate people into a coherent news product.

(Palmer, Personal communication, May 15, 2023)

Collaboration may offer more to the news consumer who may be used to watching news from different organizations than was once the case. The power of collaboration in the journalism industry is the transformative potential of collective efforts, the importance of diverse perspectives and the integrity of journalism in the digital age. The possibilities that lie ahead could include a future where collaboration is the bedrock of a vibrant and resilient journalism ecosystem.

References

CNN World Wide Fact Sheet. (February 2023). Retrieved from https://cnnpressroom.blogs.cnn.com/cnn-fact-sheet/

Egbejule, E. (2023, June 19). *I'm looking for freelancers* [Online forum comment]. Retrieved from https://twitter.com/EromoEgbejule/status/1670792555108114433

The New York Times. (2021a). International. Retrieved from https://www.nytco.com/careers/newsroom/#:~:text=International,-Members%20of%20the&text=With%20upwards%20of%20200%20international,apprised%20of%20important%20news%20overseas

The New York Times. (2021b). Journalists on the ground. Retrieved from https://www.nytco.com/journalism/journalists-on-the-ground/

Washington Post PR. (2023). The Washington Post expands global newsroom, announces new roles to grow international audience. *The Washington Post.* Retrieved from https://www.washingtonpost.com/search/?query=The+Washington+Post+expands+global+newsroom%2C+announces+new+roles+to+grow+international+audience

13 Lessons learned

Katherine C. Blair, Marion Coomey and Faith Sidlow

Figure 13.1 Global News Relay, Fresno State, California, U.S.

If you've read through thus far, you will be able to see certain themes emerge from what has been learned from the projects. It is not surprising that similar collaborative projects have faced the same challenges. If you are creating a project, here is a summary so you can anticipate what may come, or make plans to avoid such issues.

Time zones make the day much longer

The main obstacles are time zones and academic time tables. Wildly different time zones mean someone is always going to be up late, or very early if you're trying to get everyone on a call at the same time. Sometimes it is just something that needs to be done and is good preparation for a career in journalism which is anything but nine to five. Other times, communication can take place asynchronously, either through messaging, emails etc., or through leaving video or audio messages. The latter approach requires getting as much in those messages as possible to make what you have to say clear so there is no unnecessary follow-up questioning and to anticipate what the person on the other end of that message might want to know.

DOI: 10.4324/9781003428725-14

Academic timetables, term times and university policies

Academic time tables are also tricky as a number of our case studies have shown. With semester start dates sometimes wildly out of sync, the end result has often been that those countries just cannot participate. The way around this is to plan further ahead by launching a project far in advance of the beginning of your own semester to allow some contribution by others whose teaching terms may never cross over. Here, the work will be much more asynchronous, but there can still be participation in the end project. Ultimately, the project needs to work for all those involved, so if flexibility is not enough, it is up to partners whether it is worth it for them.

As well, some universities have very rigid requirements about what can and cannot be included in the curriculum and instructors do not have the flexibility to add an international project in their plans. With enough advanced planning, it is possible for those instructors to take existing assignments and adapt them to fit their university's rules.

There are also some countries that would like to participate but are constrained by governments that may restrict what students are allowed to say on camera. In one case, a university had to back out because the government was going to require the students to get permission for each and every interview they conducted and story they produced.

To assess or not

There is a contrast in approaches on whether the projects become part of assessed work or whether they are voluntary as a way of stretching the brighter, more engaged students. At Leeds Trinity University (LTU), both approaches have been tried. The students who were successful in the project, which was unmarked, were part of an extraordinary cohort who were dedicated to getting the most out of the course whether it was for marks or not, but this is rare.

Making it optional means it is difficult to predict the involvement. Some very keen students may start off full of vim and vigour, but as other pressures mount, the project is the first to go because it does not count. That approach may make the overall project unsustainable, which means all of those participating lose out.

The easiest way to get everyone on board is to build the project into assessment. If you already assess a course with a studio project, why not make it an international studio project? If you already assess video stories, why not direct your students to make them under a project theme so they can be part of an international collaboration.

At Toronto Metropolitan University (TMU), the same issues around participation have been experienced. Students are less likely to put a lot of effort into assignments if they are not assessed. Therefore, grades have been incorporated into all aspects of the productions. Some students get assessed for promoting the shows on social media; others are graded for being the liaison people who stay in touch with the students in the other countries. Every job involved in developing, coordinating and producing the international shows, is assigned to students who are then graded according to the amount of effort involved.

More interaction, earlier

What the feedback shows is how much value students place on the interaction with other students. This is often seen at the end of projects where much of the hard work, done individually by students and sometimes in isolation to those working on the same project in different countries, comes to life with the final broadcast or final project.

To inject more interaction earlier in the process, we have experimented with side projects to create a space for those earlier interactions. For example, in 2021, LTU in collaboration with April de Haas from Breda University of Applied Sciences in the Netherlands created a series of opportunities for students from both countries to share story ideas. Each tutor joined the other's class via video to introduce themselves and the idea of getting the two classes to work together.

Because the classes weren't on the same day or time, the interaction needed to be asynchronous. Marks were attached to each stage and each student was required to pitch their story idea in a short video. The other country's students watched these and created a video in return with their feedback—mostly in support of the idea, sometimes offering suggestions, or asking questions which reminded the students of cultural differences when pitching ideas internationally. This meant the students weren't working in isolation—they understood at least one of the other country's perspectives, and they started to understand there were other students like them taking part and working towards the same objective. At the end of the process, in gathering feedback, the students indicated they had a thirst for furthering and deepening these international connections. They wanted even more.

At TMU and Fresno State, a similar approach was taken. A time was set up on Zoom for students to pitch their story ideas to each other and provide live feedback. When students are pressed to explain themselves, they tend to develop more cogent thoughts and ideas. It also requires students to be more concise and adapt their story ideas to a wider, international audience.

Avoid assumptions

There is always some issue which crops up during a new collaboration, which in hindsight could be avoided, so anticipating these will make the ride smoother. For example, you can never assume anything. Don't assume that because your country routinely uses pieces to camera (also known as 'standups' when the reporter or TV presenter speaks directly to the viewing audience through the camera), that all countries will. Don't assume that because reporters in your country sign off at the end of their report with their name, that other countries do that too. Don't assume that because you teach students to shoot all their own material to avoid copyright issues that this is the same in other places. Don't assume that the terminology you use will be the same everywhere; it won't! So asking for a video package may not be as understandable to someone who's used to it being called a story or a report. Add other languages into the mix and the complications can multiply.

It is especially important to have a common terminology when everyone is in the control room calling out directions during the production of the show. The student hosts, directors and all the technical staff are already excited and anxious about doing such a big project. It's confusing for everyone if they get thrown off by the use of different terminology.

More on copyright

Be aware that there are many differences between countries about copyrighted material. Some universities allow professional news clips to be included in student video stories but in other countries that is not allowed without written permission.

As well, students need to get permission to use any video they did not shoot themselves.

There are also differences in university policies about the use of interviews in video stories. In some locations, students are required to get written permission for every interview they conduct. But in other countries, that is not required.

Students often include background music in their video stories. The use of music is complicated. Music cannot be used unless it is in the public domain (there are no exclusive intellectual property rights attached).

YouTube automatically flags copyrighted music which makes it difficult for those programmes to be published on the site.

Recognising the champions

Certainly the passion for these projects comes through in the preceding chapters, and that is because the authors have experienced success, and discovered how to make learning interesting for their students. However, these same people may not always be the ones in charge of the course. When the champions of these international projects move on to other roles, or leave their institutions, very often there is no one to fill the void. Partly that is because their colleagues may not understand the benefits of what is often extra work.

Many universities do not allow for the extra planning and organisation time it takes for some projects to come off successfully, so although they're often happy to highlight the positives—internationalisation, sustainability, collaboration, diversity, etc.—they often don't support the individuals who put in the extra effort to make them happen.

The Global Reporting Program (GRP) at University of British Columbia (UBC) in Vancouver, Canada is an exception. It receives funding from a few foundations, a private donor and the university. That's rare. The other projects outlined in the case studies in this book get occasional small research or travel grants but are run almost entirely by instructors who do not receive additional pay for their work.

Most of the projects outlined in this book have websites. Without ongoing funding, websites get dropped after a certain period of time and that means all of the archived work disappears.

Another cost for collaborative projects are the studio engineers and technicians and their time. Much of the work can be done within their regular hours but because of the huge time differences around the world, some engineers and other staff have to be in their studios and control rooms late at night or early in the morning. Some universities provide overtime pay for those hours but others do not. It's not possible to produce international collaborations without technical staff. The projects described in this book have technical staff as passionate about our projects as we are and have always been willing to put in their own time to make sure our shows are successfully produced.

Until universities truly come to value this kind of internationalisation at home, although it doesn't necessarily bring in the revenue streams of international students paying large tuition fees, such projects will be undervalued.

The hardest part of collaborating is collaborating

We continue to look for ways to get the students to connect with each other on and off camera. We've created some assignments that force the students to communicate with each other. The co-interview assignment required students from one location to do an interview on Zoom alongside a student from another country. The focus of the GENII project (Chapter 6) was to pair students in one country with students in another country to work together on one story. In the GRP (Chapter 7), the students from the UBC go to another country and work directly with the student reporters there.

In the professional world, TV, Radio and podcast co-hosts work together every day, usually in the same location. They get to know each other and develop a rapport. When they are on air, if they are good at what they do, the audience can see that they are comfortable and at ease ad libbing and bantering with each other.

It's much more difficult to develop that rapport when the co-hosts are students who barely know each other and are seeing the other hosts on monitors and hearing them through earpieces. In many cases, it may be their first time hosting a show, so they are dealing with the pressure and the nervousness that comes from having to perform. As well, English is not the first language for many of the students. The result can be very awkward interactions. Sometimes hosts do not realise it's their turn to talk and there's several seconds of silence. In other parts of the show, the hosts are supposed to interact with each other but they may feel uncomfortable ad libbing and that can also result in awkward pauses in the programme.

It helps to have the student hosts meet each other using social media well in advance of the show. It's valuable to plan the parts of the show that involve interactions between hosts and most importantly, there needs to be at least one full rehearsal so the hosts can thoroughly review the script.

Unleashing positivity

There is often a lot of pressure to sell the international project to your students. Some may not understand or be able to visualise how it will all work. Some won't see the point of bothering to stretch beyond the university, or indeed the classroom, with such projects. To get students on board and for them to make the most of it, you really need to be able to sell the project and its benefits to them. Show them why it's so much fun. Collect testimonials from students on current projects to show in your first class of the new term how positive previous students have been.

Explain what's in it for them, whether it's extra marks, increased job prospects or embedding of skills. The students need to be on board; otherwise, as their tutor, you'll be dragging them through with little joy for anyone.

Get a few of your more enthusiastic students to join you in Zoom meetings with the other universities. When students get to meet the instructors and their peers from other countries, it makes them feel more connected to the project.

At TMU students from the previous year come to the first class, show their work and talk about their experience.

The experiences shared in this chapter serve as a guide to help you be better prepared when embarking on a collaborative international project. Anticipating challenges, promoting early interactions and encouraging a positive and inclusive environment goes a long way to making these projects successful.

14 Still to come…

Katherine C. Blair, Marion Coomey and Faith Sidlow

Figure 14.1

This book has looked at an array of innovative projects launched from different parts of the world that have all had the same objective—to get students working collaboratively in a global capacity. Often, these projects have been created by educators unaware of the other collaborations already existing. That was certainly the case for Global News Relay when it was launched in 2014 by Dr. Sarah Jones (Chapter 3). She was unaware of the Global Campus Studio project which began in 2000 (Chapter 2). And it was also the case when World Earth Day Live! was conceived in 2019 without knowledge of the Pop-up Newsroom (Chapter 5), the GENII project (Chapter 6) or the Global Reporting Program (Chapter 7).

In some ways, there was a lot of reinventing the wheel because these projects were conceived of and developed in some isolation. The common denominator is the positive feedback from students (Chapter 8) and the way it is interpreted by their teachers (Chapter 9) which provides a compelling argument for continuing such collaborative projects and expanding upon their strengths.

What has also become apparent is that although the pandemic meant some broadcasts could not take place due to lockdowns that forced some of us away from our TV studios, it also accelerated the integration of online tools making

DOI: 10.4324/9781003428725-15

it easier than ever for students to collaborate virtually, and both students and their teachers are more comfortable in doing so.

Not only that, the industry has also become more accepting of different ways of broadcasting. For example, pre-pandemic, the use of video calls for interviews was mostly considered unacceptable for a TV news broadcast. So-called down-the-line interviews typically took place between the studio and a crew that set up a camera in an interviewee's home or outside location and broadcast back to base often via satellite.

Now, interviews are routinely done via the interviewee's laptop or mobile phone, making use of Skype, Zoom or Teams among other technologies. Collaboration can take place on the same documents with files easily transferred via tools like Google Docs, OneDrive or WeTransfer. And video and audio are easily transferred with editing tools now cheaper and more easily accessible.

So what next?

At our international online conference *Global Broadcast and Digital Collaborations in Higher Education* in November 2021, we demonstrated how holograms could be used to present from two locations but made to look as if in the same studio. This is already done for some sports broadcasts. For example, a tennis player in Melbourne, Australia could be interviewed by pundits in London, England, but through the use of hologram technology, they all appear on the same set.

If the technology becomes more affordable, it could be the next step following online video interviews. It's already being experimented with for remote teaching (Rubinstein, n.d.). Going beyond the use of computer screens for remote learning and moving into the use of holograms can be more effective than conventional video classes. Holograms could also be used in the pre-production process allowing students to meet and discuss topics, where at present they do so through text messaging and video calls.

Eran Shapira from Tel Aviv University in Israel suggests developing a channel or a platform that many universities can use to run news stories throughout the year rather than once or twice a year.

Eran Shapira, Instructor, Steve Tisch School of Film and Television, Tel Aviv University and Kibbutzim College of Education Technology and Art, Israel

"Maybe try to do something on a different platform like Instagram or TikTok – something very quick that's easier to produce." (Personal communication, May 1, 2023).

Still to come... 121

Marcelo Moreira from Metodista University in Sao Paulo, Brazil likes the idea of bringing interview guests into the studio to interact with the hosts and develop a deeper understanding of the theme being discussed in the programme. (Personal communication, June 5, 2023)

Future international courses could also include more material about intercultural competency, what it is and how to develop it.

Sandra Whitehead, Marquette University, Madison, Wisconsin, U.S. and Rafik Hariri University Beirut, Lebanon

> I'd tell them 'When you're in this project you'll have an opportunity to demonstrate these kinds of skills, so focus on them.' But it would also go a little deeper into realising the difference between the surface differences and the value level differences or commonalities and how to get beyond the surface.
> (Personal communication, May 18, 2023)

At the time of writing, artificial intelligence is exploding, and there's no way of telling where it might take the industry next, but it's definitely making changes in our ability to communicate.

Terry Dolph, Chief Engineer, Media, Communications and Journalism Dept., CSU Fresno, California, U.S.

> Television stations, cable channels, stuff like that, aren't just the game anymore. You can have individual networks. We're seeing more live feeds, but they're going to be from different companies that have their own little streaming stations. Artificial intelligence is going to be a part of that, too. You're going to have a program that writes, produces and edits and does everything.
> (Personal communication, April 10, 2023)

Allowing for simultaneous translation in a live broadcast could mean that every student could present in their own language and be able to have a free-flowing conversation with those speaking and understanding other languages.

The projects mentioned in this book have relied heavily on English, which has meant those who do not speak English as a first language are forced to make use of subtitling. It means a lower level of comfort when presenting on television, taking part in ad-libbed conversations, or voicing television reports.

Terry Dolph, Chief Engineer, Communications and Journalism Dept, CSU Fresno, U.S.

The future looks bright. It's very exciting. Sometimes I think I was born too early because all the good stuff is happening now. AI will probably even help with translations of different languages from the different countries so you can get an instant translation. You can do your production in your native language and then have AI immediately translate it for you.

(Personal communication, April 10, 2023)

However, it's not just technology that drives change. In journalism, educators are being challenged more and more to provide a learning environment that develops a whole range of skills in their students.

"With newsrooms shrinking, increasing emphasis placed on practical experience within journalism programmes, and issues with varying quality of internships, educators have had to be creative about how they prepare students for the graduate job market" (Valencia-Forrester, 2020, p. 698).

Combined with this challenge of creating new experiential learning environments for journalism students is the goal of universities which seek to educate the global citizens of the future and not just the privileged few who take up study abroad opportunities.

Internationalisation at home "is about intentionally making the most of the knowledge and experience of diverse student and staff members to enhance the curriculum, make learning global and at the same time create international communities at home where everyone is included" (Manning and Colaiacomo, 2021, p. 8).

Combining practical projects with greater understanding of people and issues within the global village is a progressive way of arming students with not only journalistic practical skills but also more wide-ranging skills of time management, organisation, communication and cultural sensibilities. Combining the experiential with the global has also proven a good way of increasing engagement with students.

Katherine Blair, LTU

The experience of trying to create my own global network of journalism classes in order to produce *World Earth Day Live!* clashed with the pandemic which limited opportunities for academics to network at conferences, where such networks are often formed. That forced a re-think and I started to look at how relationships in other spheres develop.

I know of a number of married couples who met initially online through apps like Tinder, and I began to explore whether such a network was available to those of us in higher education, especially those who wanted to create international projects for students to collaborate.

It turns out that although some universities such as the City University of New York (CUNY) with its well-developed Collaborative Online International Learning Working Group, or DePaul University which launched its Global Learning Experience in 2013, there isn't a free mobile app that allows educators to make their own connections. So I decided to make one.

It's called Globalizer and is available on iOS and android. You can find out more at www.globalizer.co.uk Essentially, Globalizer is an app for connecting educators globally and has been designed for universities that want to internationalise their curriculum by creating global projects for students and just need a platform to find like-minded partners.

Qualitative and quantitative research (Blair, 2022) shows students engage more with the subject and improve their performance when they work with students in other countries. Working collaboratively online without having to travel is sustainable and also allows all students to enjoy the benefits not just those with the financial backing to allow for a semester abroad or their own travel. Early reviews for the app are positive.

This book has already described how international collaboration has been used in higher education over the past two decades. The same is not true for the news industry, which is still driven by competition although there are some exceptions. Where once the predominant characteristic of journalistic endeavour was to be the first to publish, changes in the news cycle, financial pressures, and the streamlining of newsrooms have started to create opportunities for collaboration among news organisations.

By pooling resources, journalists can make use of investigative techniques and provide comprehensive coverage on stories that affect people beyond borders. Collaborative journalism is increasingly being used to address complex cross-border stories that require a wide-ranging skill set from its investigating journalists. By providing opportunities while those journalists are at university, we as educators are giving them the skills they'll need to enter the industry as it evolves.

But what of the future of journalism itself? The industry is contracting in many ways. The audience is turning away from traditional platforms that include radio, television, and online news websites.

According to the Reuters Digital News Report, only 22% of people start their news journeys with a website or app (Newman, 2023). Even Facebook is now seeing a decline. Trust in news is falling, fewer online consumers access news, and those who do, do so less frequently and are less interested, with less than half saying they are very or extremely interested in news. This is down 15% from 2017 when it was 63%. Interest in news is declining in both traditional and online media sources in most countries (Newman, 2023).

So will there be a market for journalism with such declines in interest, and who will be willing to pay for it? Will networks continue to close foreign bureaus and reduce news coverage to that which is cheaper and more accessible? It's a gloomy picture.

Elise Labott, Contributing Editor Politico Magazine, Editor-in-chief Zivvy News, Former CNN Global Affairs Correspondent

I think there's going to be more micro reporting from young people on the ground wherever they are. And anybody with a cell phone and a Twitter account or a Threads account or an Instagram account or TikTok can get it out. It's going to be more diffused. Anybody with social media accounts and a cell phone camera can do their own reports or do their own writing. With the proliferation of newsletters, blogging, social media, anybody can really be a journalist. And then I think there are going to be less and less international bureaus. Maybe there's more coverage from a wider lens but probably less quality reporting (Personal Communication, July 14, 2023).

Elizabeth Palmer, CBS News, Bureau Chief Based in Tokyo

I'm not sure whether good quality general reporting is actually going to survive. I think that certain parts of society will always want good quality news, particularly international news, and the one that comes to mind is money. Financial people who make decisions that have to do with investing a lot of money will always need very high quality information, and they're willing to pay for it. So I think that financial reporting is safe; whether you're talking about a Bloomberg terminal, or Financial Times newspaper. I'm not so sure we can say that about general reporting.

(Personal communication, May 15, 2023)

Palmer's predictions came true in Canada in June 2023, when Bell Canada Enterprises (BCE), the country's largest communications company, cut over 1,300 positions including shutting down the foreign bureaus of its flagship station, CTV, in Los Angeles and London and reducing staff at the Washington Bureau (Hudes, 2023).

Around the same time, Google removed all Canadian news from its platforms because the Canadian government passed Bill C-18 (the Online News Act) which would make digital platforms pay media outlets for content they share (Djuric, June 30, 2023).

Reducing the number of reporters in foreign bureaus and removing the ability for audiences to access the news online both have a serious impact on the future of both local and international news production.

The Australian government passed similar legislation but managed to sign agreements worth $200 million in value for news organisations, resulting in new journalism jobs throughout the country. Now other countries including the U.S., UK, India, South Africa and Brazil are considering similar initiatives (Newman, 2023).

Notwithstanding the sobering realities as a backdrop to industry, the teaching experience can still be rich and meaningful for students. The collaborations described in this book show that journalism and media disciplines are already leading the way in higher education global collaboration. They go beyond country-to-country projects and are globally focused, creating opportunities that involve multiple countries. It's hoped the Globalizer app can be used to generate networks across all kinds of disciplines to extend the idea of internationalisation at home beyond journalism education.

This book, we hope, has unveiled the remarkable achievements and insights gained from global journalism collaborations within the field of journalism and communications. The positive outcomes, driven by student feedback and educator endorsements, provide a compelling case for the continuation and expansion of such initiatives.

As technology advances, new opportunities arise, and educators adapt their approaches, the potential for international collaborations in journalism and beyond is boundless. By embracing these collaborations, we empower students to thrive in a rapidly changing world and contribute to a more connected and informed global society.

References

Blair, K. (2022). Global TV projects in journalism education. *Journalism Education*, *11*(1), 42–59.

Djuric, M. (2023a). Google set to remove news links in Canada. *CTV News*. Retrieved from https://www.ctvnews.ca/politics/google-set-to-remove-news-links-in-canada-1.6461557

Djuric, M. (2023b). Searching for Canadian news? Google ready to remove links over online news act. *Toronto Star*. Retrieved from https://www.thestar.com/business/searching-for-canadian-news-google-ready-to-remove-links-over-online-news-act/article_6e099681-b5b8-5997-8274-f2f27954caf7.html

Hudes, S. (2023). BCE laying off 1,300 people, closing foreign news bureaus and 9 radio stations across Canada. *CBC*. Retrieved from https://www.cbc.ca/news/business/bce-layoffs-radio-1.6876075

Manning, A., & Colaiacomo, S. (2021). *Innovations in internationalisation at home*. Newcastle upon Tyne: Cambridge Scholars Publisher.

Newman, N. (2023). Overview and key findings of the 2023 digital news report. *Reuters Institute*. Retrieved from https://reutersinstitute.politics.ox.ac.uk/digital-news-report/2023/dnr-executive-summary

Rubinstein, D. (n.d.). *How holograms and immersive environments transform education*. Carlton University, Retrieved from https://challenge.carleton.ca/holograms-immersive-environments-education/?utm_medium=social+organic&utm_source=linkedin&utm_campaign=challenge&utm_content=post

Valencia-Forrester, F. (2020). Models of work-integrated learning in journalism education. *Journalism Studies*, *21*(5), 697–712. doi:10.1080/1461670X.2020.1719875

Index

Note: **Bold** page numbers refer to tables and *italic* page numbers refer to figures.

academic calendar 15, 47, 62
academic time tables 113, 114
ACJ *see* Asian College of Journalism (ACJ)
AI *see* artificial intelligence (AI)
Alexander, G. 108, 109, 111
Al Jazeera 59, 105, 108, 109
American University Bulgaria (AUBG) 2
And The Good News Is, GCSP show 37, 69, 97
Angus Reid Institute 61
artificial intelligence (AI) 93, 121, 122
Ashitey, A. 66
Asian College of Journalism (ACJ) 2, 17, 19, **31,** *43,* 44, 46, 51
assessment 3, 17, 26, 27, 29, 41, 47, 51, 53, 65, 66, 69, 71, 100, 114–115
AUBG *see* American University Bulgaria (AUBG)
audio 52, 86–89, 92, 94, 113, 120
awards 59

Baines, D. 2, 43–48
Bauman, S. 45
BEA *see* Broadcast Education Association (BEA)
Benavide, J. 70, 72
Binns, M. 73
Black Pete, Christmas tradition 36
Blair, K. C. 3, 22–32, 37, 40, 65–74, *75,* 78, 84, 103–125
Bowen, K. 7–8, 10, 11
Breda University (BUAS) 36, 69, 78, 84, 115
Broadcast Education Association (BEA) 1
The Business of Dying (film) 98–99

Cain, B. 22
California State University, Fresno 22, 40, 45, 87
California State University, Northridge (CSUN) 2, 44
Canadian Broadcasting Corporation (CBC) 66, 106, 110, 111
challenges 6, 7, 9–11, 14–17, 23, 46–47, 52, 53, 55–56, 62–63, 109, 110, 113; and benefits 99–101; Global Campus Studio Productions 41–42; Global e-News Immersion Initiative 55–56; Global News Relay 25–28; Global Pop-Up Newsroom 46–47; Global Reporting Program 62–63; instructor feedback 80–82; technology 90–91; University of Johannesburg *95,* 95–97
Chen, V. 70–71
"China's Generation Green", multimedia project 58
City University of New York (CUNY) 123
climate change 53, 54
climate crisis 2, 45, 46, 110
coherent global news programme 17
COIL *see* Collaborative Online International Learning
collaborative journalism 4, 123
collaborative learning and reporting model 57
collaborative model 59–60
Collaborative Online International Learning (COIL) 15, 16–18, 55, 56, 123
communication styles 10
complex collaborations 15

128　Index

Coomey, M. 2, 34–42, 66, 71, *75,* 75–94, 113–125
copyright 116
Coventry University 2, 45, *50,* 51
COVID-19 pandemic 6, 7, 15, 25, 26, 36, 40, 53, 61, 66, 67, 90, 91, 97, 100
cross-border 55–56, 123
cross-cultural communication 3
CSUN *see* California State University, Northridge (CSUN)
cultural differences 10, 27, 115

Dennison, B. 57–64
Deuze, M. 45
Dolph, T. 91, 93, 121, 122
down-the-line interviews 120
Duarte, N. 3, 5–11

Eliminate Violence Against Women and Girls 47
empowerment journalism 60
Erasmus 16, 19, 51
eSports 41
ethics and journalistic principles 51–53, 60
Eurocentric ideas and thinking 52
European Commission 16
Excellence in Journalism conference 22, 24
experiential learning 3, 6, 18, 65, 122

Facebook 2, 8, 24, 26, 39, 40, 46, 54, 66, 88, 91, 96, 124
Ferreira-Lopes, L. 7–9
The Fish You (Don't Know You) Eat, multimedia and broadcast story 58
Floyd, G. 66
Food for Thought show 36, **38–39**, 39, 67
foreign language education 6
Fragmented (film) 97
Fresno State *see* California State University, Fresno

GCN *see* Global Campus Network (GCN)
GCSP *see* Global Campus Studio Productions (GCSP)
GENII *see* Global E-News Immersion Initiative (GENII)
Giustra Foundation 61
global audience 108–109

Global Broadcast and Digital Collaborations in Higher Education 120
Global-Campus (global-campus.org) 38
Global Campus Boot Camp 100
Global Campus films 100, 101
Global Campus Network (GCN) 1, 35, 86
Global Campus Studio Productions (GCSP) *1,* 2, *5, 34, 65,* 66, 67, 75, 77, 78, 80, 82, 83, 86–88, 97, 99, 101; benefits 42; challenges 41–42; concept 34–36; process 36–41
global collaboration 1, 4, 22, 58, 78, 79, 125; early days of 85–86
global competency 5, 15, 16, 18, 19
Global e-News Immersion Initiative (GENII) 2, 7, *50,* 50–51, 117, 119; benefits 54–55; challenges 55–56; concept 51–53; process 53–54
Globalizer 123, 125
global journalism collaboration 125; challenges associated with virtual exchange and 9–10; defining virtual exchange and 6–7; dimensions of virtual exchange and 7–9; student sentiments towards virtual exchange and 10–11
global journalism norms and practices 63
globally dominant model of journalism education 44
global news agenda 20
global news, for global audience 108–109
Global News Immersion Lab (GNIL) *see* Global e-News Immersion Initiative (GENII)
Global News Relay (GNR) 1–3, 14, 15, 17–19, *22,* 22–23, 51, 54, 67–69, 76, 87, 90, 97, 101, 113, 119; benefits 28–30, **29, 31–32**; challenges 25–28; concept 23–24; process 24–25
global partners 60
Global Pop-Up Newsroom 2, *43,* 53; benefits 48; challenges 46–47; concept 43–45; process 45–46
Global Reporting Centre 59
Global Reporting Program (GRP) 57, *57,* 80–82, 117, 119; benefits 63–64; challenges 62–63; collaborative model 59–60; concept 58–59; process 60–62
global university partners 62
GNR *see* Global News Relay

Google Classroom 9
Google Drive 25, 37, 54
Google Hangouts 24
Google Meet 24
Google News Lab 1, 54
GRP *see* Global Reporting Program (GRP)
Grunberg, R. 1, 86, 87
The Guardian 59, 110

de Haas, April 75, 78–79, 84, 115
Haivision 40, 86
Haque, S. 19
Hernandez, V. 104, 106
Higgins, L. 9, 10
Hilliker, S. M. 9
HKBU *see* Hong Kong Baptist University (HKBU)
homelessness 3, 23, 37
Hong Kong Baptist University (HKBU) 3, 25–27, 30, **38,** 67, 79
Horsfield, J. 73

ICIJ *see* International Consortium of Investigative Journalists (ICIJ)
ICTs *see* Internet communication technologies (ICTs)
immersive experiential learning 3
independent journalism organization 59
industry 103; appetite for news 106–107; collaboration 109–112; global news for global audience 108–109; journalism landscape 103–105; news production 106; 24/7 news cycle 107–108
in-person internationalization strategies 6
institutional partners 15
instructor feedback 75–84
international: audience 42; collaboration 3, 9, 18, 37, 41, 65, 82, 92, 98, 114, 117, 123, 125; group 101; learning 15, 55, 123; programme 71; reporting 7, 55, 58; student trips 51
International Consortium of Investigative Journalists (ICIJ) 109
internationalisation 5, 15, 17, 55, 117, 122, 125
'internationalisation at home' movement 15
internationalised curriculum 4, 9, 17, 78, 123
international online collaboration competencies (IOCCs) 9

International Reporting Program (IRP) 58
International Women's Day 2, 43, 45, 46
International Year of Indigenous Languages 97
Internet communication technologies (ICTs) 6, 9
investigative reporting 55, 58, 109, 110, 123
IOCCs *see* international online collaboration competencies (IOCCs)
IRP *see* International Reporting Program (IRP)

Jenzer, S. 106, 110, 111
Jesmond Local hyperlocal journalism project 44
Jonathan Logan Family Foundation 61
Jones, S. 2, 14–20, 22, 23, 30, 119
journalism: education 3, 18, 44, 52, 65; landscape 103–105; solutions 3, 28, 45; students 10, 11
journalistic principles and ethics 51, 52

Kapoor, V. 60
Klein, P. 57–64
Kolm, A. 9

Labott, E. 107–108, 124
Lam, J. 30, 75, 79
learning curve for students 91–92
learning management systems (LMSs) 9
Lebanon 2, 8, 45, 50, 53, 76, 82, 121
Leeds Trinity University (LTU) 3, 5, 26, 37, 40, 67, 68, 72, 73, 78, 84, 85, 87–89, 92, 114, 115, 123
Leilani, A. 23
Let's Talk Racism, GCSP show 36, 38, 66
Levy-Collins, G. 68
LMSs *see* learning management systems (LMSs)
"Local voices, international perspectives," GCN motto 35
Loranc, B. 9
Lord, A. 67
LTU *see* Leeds Trinity University (LTU)

Manipal University 19
Marquette University 45, 76, 79, 80, 82, 83, 121
McCullough, M. 8
McGrory, G. 68
mental health 26, 61, 67

130 Index

Metodista University 37, 77, 78, 81, 83, 121
Microsoft Teams 24, 26
Middleweek, B. 10, 11
Mind Matters show 26, 67
Mindset Foundation 61
Moreira, M. 75, 77, 78, 81, 83, 121
Morton, P. 68
Müller, E. 2
multimedia content 51, 54
multinational employers 16

neoliberalism 55
The New York Times 59, 107
Nigg, N. 28, 29

Ofcom's News Consumption 14
online collaboration 9

Painting Hope (film) 97
Palmer, E. 106, 124–125
Panama Papers 7, 109
parachute reporting 58
Paradise Papers 7, 110
peer to peer education 102
physical mobility 15
Pietraszek, W. 69
Poort, D. 105, 109
Pop-Up Newsroom *see* Global Pop-Up Newsroom
poverty 3, 22, 23, 44–46, 54
practice-based learning 35
professional broadcasters 86
professional newsroom 41

qualitative and quantitative research 123
Qualtrics survey 54
Quicklink 87

Rafik Hariri University 27, 45, 50, 76, 79, 80, 82, 83, 121
Rajaram, D. 2, 19, 43–48
Rajasekar, P. 2, 50–56
Reuters Digital News Report 124
Riley, A. 73
Rogers, B. 73
rolling news channel 15
Ryerson, E. 34, 86
Ryerson University *see* Toronto Metropolitan University

SABC Education 101
SACU *see* Southern African Customs Union (SACU)

Salford University 17, 22, 23, 30
Saltzis, K. 15
scheduling meetings 9
Scully, T. 71
Shapira, E. 75, 75, 77, 78, 81, 120
Shekarchi, A. 71
Sidlow, F. 1–4, 22–32, 40, 103–125
Sierra, J. 9, 11
simulated learning 18
Singleton, T. 105–106, 108, 109
Skype 8, 22, 24, 25, 40, 87, 88, 90, 120
Slack 8, 25
social media platforms 8, 26, 43, 105–107
solutions journalism 3, 28, 45
Soo-Yi, C. 82
Southern African Customs Union (SACU) 96
The Speech of Freedom 97
Stanford Online Platform 9
Stream Learn 101
streamline communication 24
StreamYard 26
student engagement 14–20
student group contracts 7
student perspectives 65–74
study abroad 6, 15, 70, 122
subtitles 37, 38, 40, 93
sustainability 53, 55, 117

Taras, V. 7
technology 3, 15, 30, 35, 40, 51–53, 55, 82, 87–88, 107; adapting during pandemic 88–89; challenges 90–91; early days of global collaboration 85–86; learning curve for students 91–92
Tel Aviv University 75, 77, 78, 81, 120
text-based web services 8
time difference 28, 107, 117
Toronto Metropolitan University (TMU) 1, 34, 34, 41, 65, 66, 67, 71, 86, 88–93, 114, 115, 118
trans-global collaboration 47
TV newsdays 26
Twitter 2, 26, 44–46, 66, 105, 108, 124

UBC *see* University of British Columbia (UBC)
UCT *see* University of Cape Town (UCT)
UJ *see* University of Johannesburg (UJ)
Under Pressure (film) 99
University of Alabama 22
University of British Columbia (UBC) 57–62, 81, 117

Index 131

University of Cape Town (UCT) 96
University of Johannesburg (UJ) *95*, 95–97
university policies 114

ValuePulse 9
VE *see* virtual exchange (VE)
virtual assignments 4
virtual exchange (VE): challenges associated with 9–10; defining 6–7; dimensions of 7–9; student sentiments towards 10–11
virtual mobility 15, 16
The Virtual Newsroom 35
virtual planning and brainstorming 53
virtual time converter 25
Vollenhoven, S. 95–102

Wall, M. 2, 44
WeChat 8
well-crafted social media plan 25

WhatsApp 8, 24, 25, 54, 110, 111
Whitehead, S. 27, *75,* 76, 79, 82, 83, 121
Willett, M. 26, 85, 87–89, 91, 92
de Wit, H. 15
Withers, B. 87–93
WJEC *see* World Journalism Education Congress (WJEC)
World Earth Day 3, 66, 87, 119
World Earth Day Live! 3, 65, 119, 123
World Journalism Education Congress (WJEC) 14, 15, 44

X *see* Twitter

Yoo, C. *75,* 80, 81
YouTube 2, 17, 24, 26, 28, 39, 40, 65, 91, 108, 109, 116

Zoom 8, 24, 25, 36, 40, 50, 66, 77, 80, 85, 87–90, 93, 115, 117, 118, 12

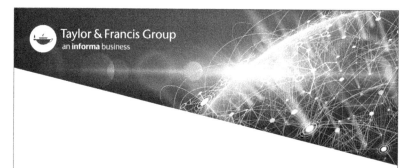

Printed in the USA
CPSIA information can be obtained
at www.ICGtesting.com
LVHW011817041124
795688LV00003B/229